DANCING
AROUND
THE EDGE

Also by Aimee Bratt

———

Glamour and Turbulence: I Remember Pan Am, 1966-1991

The Other Side of Stardom

Diplomat, Poet, Gentleman: My Father

DANCING AROUND THE EDGE

A Memoir by
Aimee Bratt

To my family and friends

Contents

Preface

Dancing Around the Edge is an imaginative description of my life's journey. From an early age, I grew up in different parts of the world, as my father was a diplomat. I attended a variety of schools, learned foreign languages, and adapted to the cultures of Africa, Europe, and the Middle East.

As a child and teenager, I enjoyed the privileged lifestyle that the diplomatic world offered, but when I returned to my native country, Sweden, I experienced a painful alienation, as if I had no roots. At the age of sixteen, I felt like an outsider. There was a barrier or edge I could not penetrate, nor did I have the desire to. I felt maladapted, and felt no love for this cold northern country.

As the years went by, however, I grew more comfortable with my surroundings and came to relish my role as an "outsider." I am sure many people feel this way now, in the multicultural world of the twenty-first century.

Once I left Sweden, I began to enjoy my experiences and adventures all over the world. I found myself "dancing around the edge," not really belonging anywhere but feeling free, strong, and self-assured. What follows here is a colorful description of the scenery that unfolded before my eyes, and stories of my participation in it.

This is an autobiography with minor fictional alterations.

Aimee Bratt, 2021

Chapter One

The Moment on the Quay

1946 ATLANTIC CROSSING

I was three years old and already mad at the world.

I did not want to pose for the photographer, and stood pouting sullenly into the camera and clutching my little lamb toy made of soft wool. My mother insisted upon tying the ribbons of my light blue felt hat under my chin a little too firmly. She gave me a lollipop, but I was in no mood to just stand there unmoving for several minutes while the photographer adjusted his equipment and gave polite directions.

There we were: little me and my family, including my mother, my older brother, and my glamorous aunt Ingrid. We stood on a pier in the New York harbor preparing to board the Swedish Transatlantic ship *Gripsholm* bound for Sweden. The year was 1946. World War II had ended but, in spite of the Allies' victory over the Nazis, the world was still in turmoil and a journey across the Atlantic Ocean could be dangerous, though not as perilous, as our crossing to the United States in December 1943, in the middle of raging war.

This moment on the quay provided me with my first real memory.

In the photograph, my mother, who was around thirty at the time, is dressed in a black skirt, white blouse, and a 1940s hat with a net in front and a huge silk flower to the side. She smiles into the camera looking very young and happy. My

The moment on the quay.

Ingrid as Stockholm Lucia, 1932.

aunt is wearing a high-buttoned, long-sleeved, light-colored dress with a very wide belt around her remarkable waist and a huge wide-brimmed hat framing her beautiful model face and shoulder-length hair. She had indeed been a mannequin and successful fashion model in New York a few years earlier, after having been crowned Stockholm Lucia in 1932. In fact, she'd won that competition by quite a wide margin, perhaps thanks to her shoulder-length hair, which—as evidenced in photos of the time—stood out from the bob styles of most of the girls.

Ingrid was very glamorous and had a continuous influence on me during my growing-up years. She loved me very much, having no children of her own. We would play solitaire, belly dance, and dance the rhumba to the music of the 1940s and '50s, to records we played on an old gramophone. It was great practice and certainly made our bodies graceful. Dancing—including ballet and jazz—was something I would continue to do for the rest of my life.

Back to the picture on the quay, which also included my older brother, five or six at the time. He had no problem posing happily with a fresh, somewhat cocky grin on his face. He was obviously enjoying the attention, in stark contrast to pouty me.

Where was my father, you might wonder. He was to remain in the U.S. as vice consul in New York, and wouldn't return to Sweden and the Department of Foreign Affairs until late 1947. His new assignment would be as bureau chief, and eventually he would serve as consul general in Berlin in 1951. His knowledge of various languages including Russian, and his expertise in east European affairs made him invaluable to the U.N. Bureau at that time. He had been vice consul at the Swedish Consulate in Chicago since December 1943.

On board the *Gripsholm*, a very famous person occupied the cabin right next to ours. Her name was Greta Garbo, and she was escorted by her companion, Mauritz Stiller. I am not sure whether they met or spoke to my family; my mother never offered any details—only that Ms. Garbo was referred to as "The Divine" or "The Mystical Woman." I must admit, I still don't see what was "divine" about her, although "mystical" seems appropriate. She famously wanted to be left alone, but that didn't set her apart from many Swedes, who tend to be quite private by nature.

Three years before our return to Sweden, when I was three months old, we had sailed from Gothenberg, Sweden, to the U.S. as World War II raged around us. We were on a "safe conduct" ship under the neutral flag of the Red Cross. The crossing took a whole month, due to stormy weather and a delay of several days caused by a German control station in Copenhagen, Denmark. The Germans did not want to let the Swedish editor for *Nordstiernan*, a Swedish newspaper, leave because he was a U.S. citizen. In the end, however, they relented and let him go.

It was a dangerous journey, and many cargo vessels and warships were torpedoed and sunk by the Germans. In hindsight, it seems questionable why the Swedish foreign office would have sent my father to a post in Chicago under such circumstances.

The ship's name was *Mangalore*. At first it took a southerly route near the Azores in an attempt to avoid torpedoes. It was a very stormy passage, and the tables and chairs had to be broken down. Passengers sat on the floor to enjoy their Christmas dinner, and, believe it or not, they sang Christmas songs, told stories, and even danced from time to time.

My brother still talks about how seasick he was, adding that he wondered how Santa Claus could reach a ship in the middle of the ocean—perhaps, by swimming, he hoped. Santa Claus did come, and the gifts were doled out accordingly.

Eventually, the ship followed a more northerly route. Just south of Iceland, its keel was bombarded and we had to divert to Newfoundland. The details of what happened are a bit murky at this point, but my brother remembers arriving in Philadelphia in the late evening. The quay was all lit up, and there were many cranes loading and unloading goods. Another little incident occurred, according to a letter from my father to the Swedish vice consul in Philadelphia.

When the m/s *Mangalore* arrived, in January 1944, the sum of $160 was stolen from us—probably while our baggage was being unloaded. The vice consul agreed to look into the matter, but had no success in discovering the thief. A letter to my father, sent to him later at the central office in Stockholm, thanked him for his efforts. He would not return to the United States.

While Philadelphia was our port of entry into the United States, a letter between the Swedish foreign office and the Swedish embassy in Buenos Aires mentions that our baggage had actually been shipped through this South American port—possibly for security and insurance reasons—then offloaded and ground-shipped to Chicago, where my father and our family were preparing to settle down in Evanston. Along with my mother, my older brother, and me was Pellas Karin, a nurse from Dalarna, a Swedish province in the middle of Sweden.

Ours was a beautiful house in the suburbs, judging by the pictures I have seen. We lived there from 1944 to 1946, and my parents had a very busy life in the diplomatic community and the Swedish society and clubs in the city.

Sweden had been criticized during the war for siding with the Nazis, but here in the United States, which was more isolationist at the time, it was less of an issue, according to my father's notes in one of his memoirs.

Meanwhile, World War II was raging and the Allies were bombarding Germany relentlessly, especially Berlin. I would witness the devastation years later.

Chapter Two

The Dark Entry Stairway

1946-1948 STOCKHOLM

I t was 1946 in Stockholm, after the war. I was a little tot, so I have just flashes of memory of the apartment we were residing in on Sibyllegatan, on the East side of Stockholm. The dark entry stairway, although gloomy and foreboding like a film noir, was elegant. The world had no colors, only black and white and grey, like scenes from those post-war 1940s films. The street outside was cobblestone and black cars passed by quietly, never honking. The atmosphere was almost eerie. The ladies on the sidewalks were dressed in suits with pinched waists and peplums, open-toed high-heeled leather shoes, and always wore hats with nets on top of their neatly coiffed heads. They had gloves and handbags and seamed nylon stockings. The suits and dresses were wide-shouldered, giving them a military look, which could be very stylish depending upon one's taste. I, for one, loved the rather dramatic look of the 1940s, as opposed to the very staid, proper, and conservative fashion that came along in the 1950s.

One day my mother, clad in one of those peplum suits and a hat, was holding my hand as we walked along the sidewalk outside our apartment when we heard a screeching sound. It happened so quickly. The car sped away and there, in the gutter, lay a little boy—lifeless, blood gushing from his nose, mouth, and ears. That was my first view of a terrible tragedy

DANCING AROUND THE EDGE

and is forever embedded in my memory and on my retinas. My mother clutched my hand and led me away from the scene, but not before we stood there for a moment, frozen by the shock of seeing the life of a child stolen in a sudden, violent act.

After the incident, my mother visited the bereaved and sorrow-stricken mother of the boy several times. She was inconsolable.

In contrast to the somber atmosphere of post-war Stockholm, our apartment was bright and sunny. I remember pale yellows, pinks, and blues. According to my older brother, our family moved to Sibyllegatan 47 in the fall of 1947, as a temporary arrangement before we would be able to relocate to a villa in a suburb of Stockholm called Ängby, in the commune Bromma. As he noted, the place was on the west side of the street, between Linnégatan and Kommendörsgatan, diagonally across from an old movie theater by the name of Puck. He called it "small and crowded." We lived there for only two or three months.

At four years old, I was apparently a difficult child. I remember spankings. My mother would "swirl" me around until I could actually see stars. Eventually, it was decided that I would be sent to Gothenburg to be with my loving grandmother (my father's mother), my Uncle Martin, and his wife Stina, as well as their wonderful housekeeper, Anna. They lived in the most beautiful sixteenth-century manor by the name of Bäckebol, in Hisingsbacka, a few miles outside the city. My grandmother had bought the estate in 1943.

In the 1940s, children were disciplined strictly, and were meant to be "seen and not heard." My mother loved me very much, but those few months on Sibyllegatan did not make for a happy time. Indeed, they were the exact opposite. I left behind that dark entry stairway for a sedate and romantic six-teenth-century house full of light. Outside, under the blue sky, were green meadows, apple trees, and berry bushes. Behind the house was a little hill with a forest where trolls lurked, it was said. Nearby were farmhouses and a brook.

The name Bäckebol means "the dwelling by the brook." The most beautiful part of this place was undoubtedly the magnificent allée leading up to the house from the nearby highway. It was a treelined allée of about 300 yards. Its crowning glory, at the end of it and next to the round grass lawn in front of the house, was a 600-year-old majestic linden tree. It was like a living legend. Here, I was happy and harmonious, and what a metamorphosis. My wonderful grandmother and namesake, Amy Bratt, had a lot to do with it.

The years 1946-1950 comprised my first episode in my native country. The second would come much later, when I was sixteen and returned to Sweden after growing up mostly in East Africa, thanks to my father's diplomatic career. That second period lasted about five years, so altogether, I lived only nine years in my native Sweden—a place I never really adapted to. This was due not only to the cold climate but to the standoffish and judgmental demeanor of my fellow countrymen as I experienced them. In 1959, at sixteen years old, when I arrived in Sweden for the second time, I hated it!

Eventually, I would find myself "dancing around the edge," that is, living all over the world, including in Africa, the Middle East, and the United States. I remain grateful for all of my experiences—but the years in Stockholm were difficult. Half the year, I'd live with my parents in the city. The other half, I'd spend in Bäckebol, happy, content, and free.

During the fall of 1947, for the modest sum of SEK 110.00 (about $10,000), my parents bought a villa in

Father in the uniform of a diplomat, c. 1940.

Bromma. The address was Pilos Väg 6. It was a comfortable and roomy house in an affluent neighborhood, with a big garden surrounded by a forest and a lake.

During this time, my mother would take me to visit our great grandmother in the city. She lived in a fine old apartment in Östermalm, in East Stockholm. We were invited to tea (or perhaps it was coffee), and I was given juice. There was always a decorative display of delicious Swedish cookies, pastries, and chocolates, along with the popular marzipan, a North European temptation. My great grandmother would sit in a room welcoming her guests. I remember lots of lace-trimmed napkins, tablecloths, curtains, and pillows. There were silver pots and ornaments, and velvety cushions in black, lilac, and lavender. The chairs were gilded and straight-backed, but Great Grandmother sat on a sofa, all dressed in black. She was mild mannered and always asked my mother whether I was well-behaved and so on. The truth was, I was a difficult child, partly because I was painfully shy—so much so that it was suggested to my mother that I should see a child psychiatrist. That never took place. My mother clearly concluded, rather wisely in afterthought, that common sense would prevail. As the years went by, I managed to take care of myself in spite of the idiotic and severely intimidating child-rearing trends of the period, at home and especially in European schools.

In those days, people told children what to do and insisted it was "for their own good." These self-righteous adults somehow derived gratification from fault-finding and passing judgement. In Sweden anyway, you were supposed to behave according to general norms, and if you deviated from that, you were shunned like a pariah. If you were different in dress or mannerism, it would not do. You had to fit in. That kind of oppression has lessened somewhat over the years, probably due to the exposure to foreigners and a lot of travelling by Swedes all over the world. As for me, I navigated my way through it, but never really embraced or adapted to Sweden fully. So much for that.

Once, when I was maybe five years old, we attended our usual Christmas dinner at the elegant apartment in Östermalm that belonged to my mother's father. This was a most traditional dinner, and everyone was expected to attend—including my mother, brother, Aunt Ingid, and maternal grandmother. Or was it my grandfather's second wife, Peggy Scott? (She was a sister of the actor Randolph Scott, whom he met in Switzerland, after divorcing my grandmother.)

Grandfather—whose name was Carl Johan Robbert, would carve the roast at the head of the huge oval dinner table. He was a very temperamental sort, of Valoon heritage—from the French-Belgian province of La Valonie. The Valoons had come to Sweden in the seventeenth century and married Swedes. They were silversmiths and goldsmiths and other craftsmen. So, on my mother's side we are Valoons, known to have tempers and darker hair. My grandfather, it was said, would get furious about something during dinner and would throw down his napkin and storm out of the room, not to return for three days. My poor grandmother, who was a very mild-mannered and tolerant woman!

They had three children: my mother, my aunt, and my uncle. My Uncle Carl emigrated to the U.S. in the 1930s and became a very successful businessman. He married my American Aunt Lois and had three children, Anna Lisa, Ingrid and Bengt. Like me, Uncle Carl was not so fond of Stockholm and lived in the States almost his entire life.

As I said, my grandfather could be very intimidating, though I barely remember him. I know that he was a very suc-

Father, c. 1950.

cessful businessman in Stockholm and moved in prominent circles of high society. My grandmother Ragnhild (from whom I get my middle name) put up with his infidelities and tantrums until their ultimate divorce. Grandfather and Peggy Scott had two sons together, Eric and John. John perished in an auto accident in California, and Eric became a successful silversmith and, after three marriages, moved to Greece.

I met Peggy only once, in Stockholm, at the opulent Östermalm apartment. Her son Eric was present, and I remember that he berated her a little over her drinking. In spite of it, she retained the finishing-school mannerisms of a true Southern belle.

My grandfather was an avid marksman. So the story goes, he perished accidentally, when he was cleaning his rifle and it went off and shot him. The truth is, he committed suicide. Perhaps his bad temper finally got the best of him, but we'll never know for sure. The tragedy occurred in the early 1950s, when we were no longer in Sweden.

Chapter Three

The Yellow House by the Brook

1946-1950 BÄCKEBOL

äckebol was situated in Hisingsbacka, a borough north of Gothenburg, Sweden's second largest city. All around it, farmhouses spread out against the surrounding woods. There was only one highway, about a mile away, where one could take the local bus to and from the city. In the 1940s there was not much motor traffic, and people would walk or bicycle to get around. Bäckebol was the most beautiful old house, about the size of a manor and built in 1764 by a prominent man by the name of Johan Oliveholm—although the estate is documented as far back as 1642, when it was owned by a Danish nobleman and Sweden belonged to Denmark and Norway. He and many of the subsequent owners are buried in a private cemetery in Backa, about a ten-minute walk from the house. Both my father and my mother are buried there, as well as my grandparents.

My grandmother, Mrs. Amy Bratt, bought Bäckebol in 1943, the year I was born, and had it thoroughly restored. Her father, C.L. Berggren, had managed the estate while the owner was living abroad. My Uncle Martin and his wife Stina became its owners after my grandmother's death. They lived there until my uncle died suddenly in his mid-eighties, after which my aunt Stina moved elsewhere. Bäckebol was subsequently sold and is no longer in the family. It is, however, a cherished memory and, for me, represents a special place in Sweden where I spent my happiest times as a very young child.

In 1964, Bäckebol was declared a historical building by the Swedish Board of Antiquities, which means that neither its interior nor its exterior may be altered. To this day, driving up to the house it feels like stepping back into the nineteenth century.

So this was the house where my grandmother Amy, my uncle Martin, and my Aunt Stina lived for many years. My mother, father, and I intermittently stayed there for visits, which were by far the best ones in my native country.

The serenity of the place was something I would never again experience in my lifetime, and it had a special kind of mystery, something out of a tale of times gone by, with hidden secrets in the attic and cellar and in the woods behind the house where the trolls were said to dwell.

My grandmother was the embodiment of kindness, gentility, and civility. She almost never uttered the word "no." It was, "Yes, my dear," and "Of course you may," which, as a three to five-year-old, I would take advantage of. My mother loved her endlessly, and described her as self-effacing—but don't get the wrong idea: She was ever so intelligent. Having been bred in the Victorian fashion, which was prudish and judgmental, she was nonetheless warmhearted, tolerant, and patient with just about everybody. She died in the same room where she had been born—the so-called stone parlour or *stensalen*. It was a very elegant room with a piano, antique furniture, paintings of kings and queens, and a floor clock from an era gone by, which would chime every half hour.

My grandmother's name, Amy, is Victorian—derived from the French *Aimee*. During that era, everything French was admired and copied, so *Aimee* was anglicized to *Amy*. (I myself use both names, depending on the situation. For example, when

Bäckebol entrance (exterior).

I was in show business I used *Aimee,* as the more foreign-sound-ing spelling seemed beneficial in trying to get cast in New York.)

My great grandmother's name was Ellen Birch (Ellen is my second name). She was a governess until she married Carl Leopold Berggren, a well-to-do merchant in Gothenburg, who owned a beautiful estate by the name of Hulan outside of Falun, in the middle of Sweden.

My grandmother and I occupied the attic in Bäckebol. She slept in a little room in a high-posted bed covered with lacy sheets and quilted covers. There was a little window facing the forest behind the house, where moss-clad stone steps led up to the top of a hill and fir trees and pine trees grew all around.

I slept on a little cot in the room next to her, where I felt especially happy and secure in her unconditional love. In the evening before going to sleep, she would read to me from storybooks, and now and then, when she got a little sleepy, she would skip a page by mistake—whereupon I would call out, "Grandma, you skipped a page . . . go back!" And she did.

I took advantage of her compliant nature. I love to dance, and at that time we used to play old records on the gramophone in the library, a very big and comfortable room with a red carpet and Gustavian furniture where guests were entertained. On that big carpet, I danced and danced to the music of the 1940s, especially my favorite piece, Ravel's "Bolero." I never wanted to go to bed, in spite of my grandmother's pleas. Anna, our beloved housekeeper, would step in, insisting in her firm voice, "Now, Amy *must* go to bed!"

My love of dance, especially ballet, was a big part of my young life, wherever we lived in the world. My Aunt Stina encouraged me by giving me a pretty tutu made just for me of white satin and tulle. I was already taking ballet classes in Gothenburg, and was so good at it that I could do the splits all the way, and move around the dinner table balancing on my bare toes.

Stina was a schoolteacher in a nearby high school, and one day she invited a few of her students home. They were maybe ten or twelve years old and dressed in ballet outfits, and I was in awe of them. Later, Stina asked me if I'd enjoyed the little get together, and which one of the girls I'd liked best. I told her, and then why I had picked that particular girl. "Can't you see? She's the prettiest one!" I explained. I wanted to be just like her.

Stina and I would take long walks into the woods on little forest paths, and all around us were berry bushes of all kinds—boysenberries, lingonberries, blackberries—all of which could be picked when ripe. We would also pick lilies, violets, and marigolds. Using our imaginations, we could almost see the trolls peering at us from deep in the forest, from behind the trees and moss-covered stones.

Passing through meadows and leas and over little brooks, we would walk for about twenty minutes until we came upon a glen where cows often grazed. We'd traverse the rills on little bridges or wooden planks. Those summer days and mild evenings playing around the compounds of Bäckebol were the happiest of my childhood.

The rooms in Bäckebol dated from the seventeenth century and were all furnished with Gustavian furniture. Leading up to the house were two flights of stone steps, one leading up to the second floor and one to the front door. Inside the front door was a vestibule, which was adjacent to the stone parlor. From there, a winding, carpeted staircase of polished wood led upstairs. On the third floor were the library and bedrooms, and a special anteroom with dainty elegant tables and chairs. Its French door looked out over the linden tree, the allée, and the wide, grassy lawn. Outside that door was a wonderful and architecturally significant little balcony made of wrought iron and decorated with real cannon balls from the seventeenth century.

Behind the stone parlor was the impressive main dining room, furnished with an oval mahogany dining table. Above the table hung the most magnificent crystal chandelier you can imagine, and the walls held a variety of art. Most awe-inspiring of all was a huge oil painting of various food items: fishes, meats, vegetables, along with ewers and canteens of china. It actually took up most of the entire wall. One of the smaller pictures— an etching of a bull with fierce eyes—captivated and scared me. One day, I declared to Stina, "That picture is dangerous for children!" Even at a young age, I had a wild imagination.

Closer to the kitchen, there was yet another dining room with a large console holding an amazing array of porcelain dishes and china sets. Other cupboards held yet more beauti-

The Stone Parlor.

ful china plates, crystal glasses, and silverware that had to be polished from time to time. The chandeliers, too, had to be cleaned quite often, a painstaking procedure but that's the way it was in those times. Stina did not even want a washing machine; all the linens, towels, and sheets had to be washed by hand, mangled, and ironed with special presses in the attic!

The kitchen was the largest I have ever seen. We often took our meals there, next to two stoves and surrounded by cabinets of all kinds. At the back was a most efficient pantry, with a huge icebox and shelves laden with jams and jellies, breads and conserves, and an extraordinary variety of bottles and cans.

In this kitchen we were served breakfast, lunch, and afternoon tea, when we ate Swedish biscuits and sandwiches. Dinners were often served in the dining room. Our evening meals included elk meat and venison, potatoes, always accompanied by jelly. There were also fish dishes, including boiled cod or pike, with potatoes garnished with dill and egg sauce. Northern food is good food, tasty and always healthy, and meatballs are served with special gravy and lingonberries.

In the kitchen, after our meals, we would wash and dry the fine china dishes and place them back on their shelves. A dishwasher was unheard of, and of course there was no TV; we had conversations!

Stina had wardrobes filled with beautiful clothes, including evening dresses made of brocade, shantung silk, and velvet. She enjoyed taking these out of their storage covers and showing them to me—just for fun, never to show off. That was not Stina's way. She was a totally genuine person—honest, kind, and possessing a keen sense of humor, just like Uncle Martin. If you were to meet them, you might get the sense that they were staid and conservative, but it was quite the opposite when you got to know them. Neither of them was the least bit petty; like my father, they were ever so tolerant and mild-mannered, and like my grandmother, major influences in my life.

Perhaps now you have a sense of what life was like in Bäckebol. For me, it was a place never to be forgotten.

Chapter Four

Ängby and the Ugly Kids in School

1948-50 STOCKHOLM

After Sibyllegatan, the family moved to a sedate suburb in Bromma, north of Stockholm, called Ängby. It was a beautiful area with good houses and gardens set well apart from one another. There were very few cars there in the early 1950s, and one could bicycle along the streets and side paths. We children played anywhere we chose, including in the forest area behind our houses.

When I was six or seven years old, and about to start my first year in school, I was not particularly pretty. I had a round face, a space between my front teeth, and my hair was straight and stringy. I was also very shy. A girl named Berit who lived next door was my best friend. One day I learned an important lesson from her. Berit and I were sitting on the stoop of my house and on the ground before us were squirrels. For some really foolish reason, I picked up a stone and threw it at one of them. Luckily I missed, but Berit got very angry and scolded me. "How could you do that!" she said. I felt real shame—a kind I had never felt before. Never would that happen again, or anything like it. In that moment, I developed an unending love for all animals. It took only a few seconds, but the impact my friend had on me was significant.

One day—during the time of Stalin and the dreaded KGB—the Russians came. My father was still in the Foreign Office at the time, acting as Bureau Chief and interacting with the Russians, Germans, and British. The Russians were feared in Sweden, as they were throughout Europe, and the watchword in the Foreign Office was, "For goodness sakes, don't do anything to upset them!"

They tumbled out of their black Volga cars in rumpled baggy suits, looking just as they did in the movies. "Daddy, Daddy, the Russians are here!" cried my brother. What were they doing on our quiet little suburban street? Was it some kind of threatening business? As my father greeted them in Russian, a gift was presented to him: a case of vodka and a case of Krim wine. But the conservative Swedish Foreign Office let it be known that such favors could not be reciprocated. I think my father probably kept the presents, and, though I don't remember it, I think he invited the men in. He spoke Russian fluently, and was very familiar with Russian culture, music, and literature. He enjoyed their company very much.

During our time in Ängby, my father was deeply into writing his Ph.D. thesis, "The Minor States in the History of Antique Government Doctrine"—a *very* academic piece of work. We all understood that he was not to be disturbed in his study.

Around this time, we had our portraits made, which was typical for the time period. The artist was a Russian by the name of Boris Smirnoff. He came to our house and did drawings in pastels of my mother, brother, and Aunt Ingrid, who visited us often. The painting he did of me I did not like at all. I thought I looked very childish with my bangs hanging like a curtain around my face!

Then came the dreaded first day of school. Previously, my mother had enrolled me in a drama school for children, where I'd taken ballet classes. That dark studio somewhere in Stockholm—probably a kindergarten—had suited me much better than what was to come.

As I'd feared, my first day of school was a horrible experience. In 1950, not much attention was given to timid little girls. The boisterous boys and their rough play in the schoolyard scared me. The building was an ugly red-brick house, and my classmates were even uglier. I did not fit in at all, mostly due to my extreme shyness. The teachers were very severe and I don't remember learning much. I longed to be home with my mommy and daddy and Lisa, our German housekeeper. She had escaped to Sweden during the war, after being struck by part of a roof during a bomb attack by the Allies. She was my friend. Thankfully, that first school year came to an end when my father was appointed Consul General in Berlin.

According to my brother, we lived in Ängby from January 1947 to the summer of 1951. After that, I was free of Sweden and happier times were in my future. Except for the time I spent in Bäckebol, my memories of Sweden, if not downright unpleasant, left a negative impression I retain to this day.

My parents were the most loving any child could wish for, so there was nothing to be ungrateful for. My father, like my grandmother, loved me unconditionally, and rarely said no to my wishes. My mother was a bit more of a disciplinarian and quite parsimonious. I was allowed to wear just a few dresses and was far from spoiled—quite the contrary. This was postwar Europe, and people were thrifty. Children were strictly brought up and expected to behave themselves in school and at home. However, I knew my mother loved me very much. In later years, when she'd hear about crimes committed by children or adults, she'd say, *"Dom får ingen kärlek!"*—"That's because they get no love!"

Chapter Five

The Bungalow in Dahlem

1951-1953 BERLIN

Driving into war-torn Berlin in 1951 still haunts me with black-and-white images. There were ruins everywhere you looked, sooty facades and jagged edges of buildings that had stood erect in prosperous times.

There were large heaps of fallen bricks, deserted streets, broken pavements, and desolation. The few cars there were all black. Children stared at us with hollow eyes and old faces, clad in dilapidated lederhosen and shod in gaping old shoes and tattered socks. I will never forget the one who stuck his tongue out at us as we drove by in our 1949 Mercedes Benz. I was eight years old and could not understand this ugly gesture. Perhaps he'd have aimed it at any foreigner who happened to drive by, imagining the person's comfortable life far from the misery of East Berlin, which was in the Russian Sector.

My father's new post as Swedish consul general for Berlin came in 1951, and we'd had a harrowing drive there from Sassnitz, a German border town on the Baltic Sea. I suffered from car sickness, made worse by the acrid smell of the benzene diesel that fueled cars at the time. Almost every twenty minutes we had to stop so my mother could take me into the woods and hold my head while I got sick. The black 1949 Mercedes was not very comfortable, and the road we drove on was more of a forest path, quite bumpy, with pine trees and thick vegetation all around us.

It was five years since World War II had ended, and East Germany was occupied by the Russians and the Allies. We had no idea what awaited us up the road. As we rounded a bend, two East German soldiers jumped out of a hiding place in a tree with their rifles pointed at us. I was not really scared—mainly just bewildered.

My father stopped the car and, as I vaguely recall, spoke to the officers in German, and they allowed us to continue. It turned out we'd taken a wrong road and were in a forbidden area.

After a few more hours of grueling driving along desolate forest paths, we arrived at a Grenz station, where we were promptly halted by Russian and East German military police. This time, I was frightened as they took my father into a little guardhouse for questioning, leaving my mother, brother, and me sitting in the car, waiting.

We waited for a full two hours, as I kept asking my mother why they'd taken my father away. The anxiety of separation at my tender age was terrifying, and I had never before experienced anything of a warlike nature, since Sweden had remained politically neutral—and 'spared by the Nazis"—during the war.

Berlin in ruins.

To our great relief, my father eventually reappeared, accompanied by the guards. He was in good spirits. It turned out that, after a lot of wrangling and repeated explanations in both Russian and German, he had finally managed to convince them that he was the future Swedish Consul General on his way to his new post in Berlin. We'd been driving the wrong way through the woods, and had found ourselves on a "refugee road," a path well known to the Russians. Having explained our presence, we were then allowed to continue to Berlin. The road remained in terrible condition and at one point, according to my brother, we drove right into a giant hole. I have no recollection of that. I only remember how carsick I was from the diesel fumes.

The Allies had divided Berlin into four sectors. The American, British, and French sectors were in West Berlin and the Russian sector was in East Berlin. The latter was very poor and desolate, and the stream of refugees from there was endless.

The cold war was ongoing and, according to my father's memoirs, the Soviets were afraid of the development of a separate German State. Although Berlin was isolated and one of the most militarily, politically, and geographically vulnerable spots in Europe, it was still able to retain its pre-war stature as a metropolis. Surprisingly, there emerged a boost in morale, which was normalizing and refreshing. This post-war atmosphere in Berlin became almost glamorous in its optimism; international society was thriving. There were black-tie parties, garden parties, and cocktail parties. I watched the grown-ups. They were elegant in the way they carried themselves and spoke, displaying their international education and sophistication. Just as in the movies of that era, there was a lot of martini-drinking and cigarette-smoking! My mother had a seamstress,who came to the residence and made clothes for

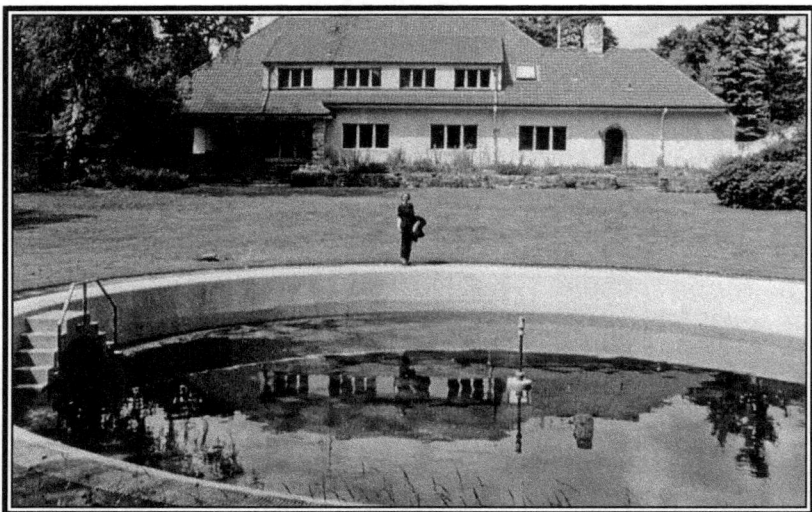

The house in Dahlem.

her: dresses in satin and brocade with halter tops like the ones worn by Ava Gardner and Lana Turner in their films.

We settled into a beautiful house on Pücklersstrasse in Dahlem, the American sector. This was the Swedish consulate residence and displayed the consulate emblem on its front entrance. The streets were tree-lined and every other house was an American bungalow with an ample, well-manicured garden. We had a huge, completely round, old-fashioned swimming pool below the large grass lawn where the garden parties were held.

There was a little brook with weeping willow trees bending over it. Behind our house was Grünewald, a forest, and amongst the trees were ruins where children played in spite of the danger that they might come crashing down. Our house was the last one on the block, and next to us was one of those ruins—a very large one.

On a day I will never forget, like many German children at that time, I was rollerskating on big, heavy "rollshuen" with my little friends. Suddenly, in front of our eyes, the pine trees next to the ruin started to sway menacingly, and with a tremendous roar like thunder, the structure came crashing down. It took perhaps a full minute. Luckily, no one got hurt, but it was a strange and awesome sight.

The house on Pücklersstrasse was a two-floor bungalow with a very wide flight of stone steps leading down to the lawn in back. Besides holding garden parties there, we played badminton and swam in the magnificent pool. The setting was ideal for playing hide-and-seek and other imaginative games—so we did.

I made a best friend named Anita Heiliger, who lived in Grünewald with her parents in what can only be described as a hovel. Her father was a sculptor, always hacking away at stone figures, and they were dirt poor. After the war, which devastated much of the population, many eked out a living any way they could. Their ability to survive had been tested, and there was much suffering in the aftermath of the relentless bombardment of the Allies. Many, like our Ängby housekeeper Lisa, fled to Sweden to work as domestics.

Anita's mother was the most bohemian character I had ever met. She was thin and blond and played solitaire constantly with the dirtiest little heap of playing cards I had ever seen. At their house, we'd make sandwiches of lard and salt on dark German rye that was so hearty it was almost like eating tree bark. Amazingly, once I got used to these snacks they actually tasted good! Anita had long blond hair like mine, and like all little girls, we would put our heads backwards and compare who had the longest and fullest tresses.

Anita was quite obstinate and had a habit of announcing boldly, "*Unser ist viel besser!*"—"Ours is much better," whatever the item was. Since, in her eyes, I was a privileged kid and she was poor, she must have felt the need to assert herself in this way. It was a curious kind of confrontational "payback" often demonstrated by the Germans at that time, perhaps a sign of their insecurity at having lost the war. They were bad losers; even at my young age I could see it clearly.

My second school year would be much more pleasant than my first had been. There was a Swedish church in Berlin, and on its property was a school for Swedish children. There were so few of us in each grade, we all in the same room and had the same teacher, who was excellent. We learned easily and quickly, and received a lot of individual attention—almost like tutoring. Before long, I had learned to speak German fluently.

Working for us were our housekeeper, Martha, her assistant, Hedy, and the chauffeur, Bosacker. From them, I quickly adapted to the Berlin way of speaking. There was warmth and laughter in our house, and I amassed a lot of pleasurable memories. Wonderful ham sandwiches were prepared for me to take to school, and Bosacker, a feisty and jovial character, would drive me there every morning.

I continued my study of ballet and danced in our living room to the tunes of the fifties, played on the old gramophone just as in Bäckebol. I was always balancing on my bare toes and dancing around the dining table. I did, of course, acquire ballet slippers along the way, and they would constantly wear out and require mending.

One day in 1953, as we sat down for lunch, my father made a big announcement: We were going to Africa! He had gotten a new post as a Swedish envoy (called a minister in those days) in Addis Ababa, Ethiopia. Today the title *minister* is not used anymore; it's all about ambassadors.

So, our future lay in Africa, and what a journey that would become! Never could I have imagined what adventures and exotic experiences were ahead of me, and how they would shape my view of the world. The insights and cultural lessons I would learn would last throughout my life. The 1950s in East Africa would become known as the golden age, and, in a way, I feel I am still there; it is under my skin.

I really believed my African dream would never end, but—like all things—it eventually did, in 1959. My years there, from 1953 to 1959, were the most formative of my life, and the most significant. My entire outlook on the world, both socially and culturally, came into focus during that time.

As we proceed, I will try to describe the beauty, adventure, and mystery that became Africa to me.

Chapter Six

The African Dream that Could Never End

1953-1959 ETHIOPIA

Ethiopia, formerly known as Abyssinia, is an ancient region in the "Horn of Africa," bordered by Sudan to the east and the Gulf of Aden and Indian Ocean. To the north are Egypt and Eritrea, a confederate state of Ethiopia whose capital is Asmara. The name Abyssinia was derived from *Abesh*, meaning mixed people and races, i.e., Hamite, Semite, and African. The country was occupied by Mussolini and Fascist Italy from 1936 to 1941, during World War II.

Ethiopia's capital is Addis Ababa, which sits at an elevation of 8,000 feet in a very mountainous region similar to that of Mexico City. The country's beautiful scenery consists of craters from extinct volcanoes, deep canyons, and cone-shaped mountains that appear like moonscapes in the north. In the south are large lakes and acacia groves populated by flamingoes and pelicans. In the east are savannahs with hordes of gazelles and antelopes, and in the west a more lush terrain, like that of Central Africa.

It is a biblical land, where the Queen of Sheba once ruled. In the 1950s, reminders of its ancient culture were all around us: women clad in their *shammas*—white loin cloths with colorful borders; sprawling cottages; carriages led by "gary" horses, which served as local transportation, and,tragically, as in the Bible, people afflicted by leprosy begging in the streets.

This was long before the Marxist revolution of the 1970s, and Ethiopia was a feudal country. The Amharas were the ruling class and land owners, and had all the power. (The title *Ras* means *noble*, and many of these Ethiopians had this title.) The emperor was Haile Selassie, a descendant of the Meneliks and thus of Menelik II, Emperor of Abyssinia from 1889 to 1913. He was the most mild-mannered and gentle human being— not at all the despot he was accused of being later on, by revolutionaries who wanted to seize his power and eventually murdered him. (More about him later.)

The clergy had a lot of power, just as they had had in medieval Europe. The church was Coptic Greek Orthodox, and its priests wore colorful robes and headgear. For the Mascal, a religious celebration of sorts, all the priests would gather in the main square of the city and sing their mantra songs and dance. It was all very colorful—an awesome sight to behold.

Then there were the shop owners and tradesmen. They made up the third class of this feudal society, and were mainly Italians who had settled there during the occupation. There were also Armenians and some Greeks. In the countryside were typical little "Mom and Pop" Italian restaurants with white-washed walls and grapevines, where one could eat old-fashioned macaroni with meat sauce and parmesan cheese out of large soup bowls, accompanied by red Chianti wine. Oh, was it good!

The final and fourth feudal class consisted of the natives, who were spread out all over the country. These were members of the Galla and Oromo tribes, who barely eked out a living in the wilderness. They wore animal hides and made jewelry—bracelets, necklaces, and so on—out of materials they found in the villages and from the cans we discarded when we went into the bush on the outings that were such a wonderful part of living in Africa at that time. These natives hunted with spears and grew their own crops to survive. They were always peaceful and gentle, smiling as we, the "aliens" from another, tried to converse with them a little. They spent hours just looking at us as we put up our tents and prepared our overnight quarters with all the paraphernalia we'd brought in our Land Rovers and Jeeps.

These native people were used to the missionaries who had lived in Ethiopia since the nineteenth century, and had set up schools and makeshift hospitals as part of their efforts to convert the locals to Christianity. They mostly succeeded.

We Swedes called our home *Addis*, whether we had been invited there by the emperor to assist and aid his country or appointed by the Swedish government to do the same. The Swedish colony consisted of about 500 people: teachers, engineers, aviators, doctors, nurses, judges, police instructors, army officers, telecommunications experts, and other professionals.

According to diplomatic protocol, my father had arrived three months before we did. Our flight to Addis was bumpy, and of course I was airsick. I believe the airline was Transair, a Swedish charter company that flew DC-6s from Sweden with a transit stop in Rome. The flight over the mountains of Ethiopia was extremely turbulent, and we could hear our German shepherd, Suzy, barking in her cage in the airplane's belly. As we looked down over Addis Ababa, a sprawling village with both Western and Ethiopian features, we saw white-washed huts intermingled with European-style stone houses with corrugated sheet-metal roofs.

In 1953, the airport was nothing more than military barracks. When we stepped out of the plane, we were met by a few Swedish representatives and our chauffeur, who would drive us to the legation, as it was called at that time. The Swedish flag on the car was not displayed, as it was reserved for ceremonial and official business events.

The Swedish legation was a yellow stone building that had been constructed in the Italian style during the Mussolini occupation. It sat on a hill, surrounded by a park and a garden, and had two entrances, the main one and another at the upper end of the compound with the Swedish royal emblems on the gates. There was a stone wall all around the area, a grass lawn in front of the house, and flowers and trees lining a gravel path.

This beautiful place would be my home for the next six years—really, the only true home I would ever know. A staff of maybe twelve servants, employed by the Swedish government, greeted us. There were the gardeners, the gate guards, and the stable man (we had six horses) to take care of the outside; and the cook, kitchen help, and two household servants inside. There was also a porter for the office on the bottom floor, where my father and his secretaries worked; a chauffeur; and later, a nanny for my brother who was yet to be born.

The legation was furnished with 1950s-style sofas, chairs, tables, and lamps—the kind you see in movies of that time. The upholstery was sateen, the wood mahogany, and the carpets oriental. The lamps in the ceiling would eventually be riddled with termites! The décor was very Swedish, meaning it was quite spartan compared to the more posh and luxurious interiors of the French, British, and Italian embassies. My mother used to complain about that. Anyway, it was elegant enough as a Swedish legation to host many cocktail parties, receptions, black-tie dinners, and garden parties.

In the stairwell leading up to the bedrooms was an imposing painting of the Swedish king, Charles XII, as a twelve-year-old lad but looking much older. He died in the Battle of Poltava in 1812, when the Swedes fought the Poles. I never

The Swedish Legation in Addis.

forgot this particular date from my history lessons.

At ten years old, I was now experiencing the uncomfortable affliction of altitude sickness. At 8,000 feet the air is thinner, and the lack of oxygen can make one quite ill, at least temporarily. It took me about three months to get over my nausea and become accustomed to the altitude.

Upon our arrival, I was promptly placed in the Swedish missionary school that adjoined the Swedish church, in an arborous setting up on a hill about a twenty-minute car ride from the legation. Every morning, our chauffeur would drive me there in the Jeep. This was fun for me, because he was a really nice man and taught me some Amharic: words such as *tanasterling*, the usual formal greeting, and *egzjabersterling*, which literally means "God will reward you" but is used to say thank-you. He taught me the words *ante* (man or boy) and *antchie* (woman or girl) and *bbrr* (silver or money). I learned more words from my Ethiopian friends as the years went by.

My memories of Ethiopia—the "golden age" of my youth—are forever cherished. "Once Africa, always Africa," as

Haile Selassie and my father, c. 1956.

the saying goes. While I lived there, I wasn't "dancing around the edge" because Ethiopia was where I felt rooted and at home there. In fact, I never thought I would leave. Inevitably, however, that life did end.

I don't think I ever fully recovered from the shock of being separated from the secure and protected environment of this beautiful East African country in the mountains. As an idealistic teen, I'd felt shielded from the rest of world there.

Haile Selassie, the "Lion of Judah," was the identity of his country. In 1936, he made a dramatic plea to the League of Nations—the body that would become the United Nations—to save his country from the invasion of Mussolini. Shamefully, his entreaties were met with indifference. It seemed that no one of any importance cared about this remote East African country.

My father had many meetings and visits with Haile Selassie, about which I have written in my book *Diplomat, Poet, Gentleman: My Father*. My own encounters with the emperor and empress took place at the yearly Christmas parties held for the international community's children. I remember that at one of these, my mother and I were placed in a long procession along with all the other diplomats' family members. Slowly, we all walked up to the emperor and empress, who were seated on their thrones. I had been instructed in how to curtsy all the way to the ground, and that's what I did. As I took the gentle hand of Haile Selassie, he asked me sweetly, "Do you speak French?"

"No, just English," I replied.

He smiled and I moved on to the empress, who greeted me weakly. She was very ill at the time, with complications from diabetes. After the introductions, Santa Claus arrived in a helicopter that seemed to come from heaven above, and all of us children got lavish gifts!

The emperor was diminutive in stature and most dignified, his eyes melancholy and searching. He had visited Sweden once, before becoming emperor, and the Swedes had a very favorable opinion of him, especially in light of the shabby treatment he'd gotten in 1936, at the League of Nations.

Whenever the emperor left or returned to Addis Ababa, he and his entourage would pass beneath elaborate triumphal arches. His people would throw themselves to the ground in his honor. This may seem highly undemocratic but, as I have said, Haile Selassie was a benevolent ruler. He abolished the Friday hangings of his predecessors, and strove to improve his ancient and under-developed country as best as he could, inviting Americans and Europeans to assist his country with their expertise. The term *third world* was not yet in use, and the Swedes referred to Ethiopia as a U land.

The fact that Haile Selassie may have had money stashed away in a Swiss bank prompted his enemies to label him corrupt and despotic. In their hunger for power, they eventually murdered him—allegedly by suffocation with a pillow.

My memories of Haile Selassie and my father's reverence of him are captured in the beautiful picture I have of the two of them.

In 1956, after a few years at the Swedish missionary school, I was too senior to continue there. I graduated with very fine grades in English, Swedish reading and writing, the scriptures, mathematics, geography, history, science, art, signing, and sports—every class included in the curriculum at that time.

I had no choice but to try the French lycée up the main road in Addis Ababa. International children were first accepted into the

Classe d'Accueil, a welcoming of sorts and introduction to the main school. We were taught as much French as possible, so that we'd be prepared for the lycée—which would turn out to be nothing short of a nightmare for me. But I enjoyed the preparatory school, mainly because of a very kind and tolerant teacher who guided us through the rather difficult process of learning French properly. As I recall, she had very bad eyesight and wore heavily rimmed glasses, but was nonetheless an attractive blond woman.

When *Classe d'Accueil* came to an end, we were transferred to the hellish lycée, housed in a yellow stone building with a huge front yard where all these rowdy kids ran around yelling. The first day, I was placed somewhere in the back of the classroom, not knowing what to expect. I was bewildered and wanted to run away.

The French teacher made his entrance, looking very severe. He did not pay any attention to us newcomers, just started speaking very quickly in French, and of course I did not understand a word. After addressing one of the boys and not getting the response he wanted, he delivered a violent blow to the boy's face. It sounded like the lash of a whip! I was in shock, and remember coming home crying, never wanting to set foot there again. My father immediately relented and it was decided that we would try the English school. I have no idea why we hadn't tried that in the first place.

At the English school, I fit right in and was happy—very happy. It was so civilized and "British" there; the classes had names such as "Remove A," "Remove B," "Certificate A," and "Certificate B." My fellow pupils were between the ages of twelve and sixteen and of all nationalities: English, German, Japanese, Italian, Greek, Armenian, American and, of course, Ethiopian.

The curricula were Geography, History, English Composition and Literature, Math, Science, and Scriptures—the last of which was taught by an American woman. (From history class there, I still remember the date of the Battle of Hastings: 1066.) We had many lessons on Shakespeare, learning long monologues by heart and performing his works. Looking back, I think we were probably too young to really understand that kind of drama.

We put on school plays frequently, and—perhaps because of my long blond hair or because of my father—I was often cast in the lead role of a princess or something of that nature. I had many lines to learn, but I did my best. Once, the headmaster, who was standing far away from the stage, could not hear me as I spoke. He called out a bit sarcastically, "I can't hear a word…what language is that?"

The headmaster was a very good-looking Englishman, in contrast to his very frumpy wife. I could not understand their relationship at all, and I suspect theirs was not a happy marriage.

I was still very shy, but managed to get good grades and many complimentary comments on my reports. At that time, pupils were scrutinized and judged very thoroughly. At the bottom of one of my reports, the headmaster wrote, "This is excellent. I am very pleased to see how Amy has settled down. She is a most promising pupil." The geography teacher commented, "Has done extremely well in her short time here. A very intelligent girl." There were other accolades as well.

Since childhood, I have always gotten along very well with English-speakers—the British and the Americans—almost as if I were one of them and not Swedish-born. For one thing, I appreciate the fact that they pronounce my name correctly!

We had school dances where we danced to the tunes of Elvis Presley and Fats Domino, intermingled with Ethiopian music. To "Rock around the Clock," "Jailhouse Rock," and

"Blueberry Hill," we'd do the jitterbug, then move seamlessly on to the rhythmic Ethiopian music. It was great to be fifteen years old and dancing into the night!

There was an embarrassing moment at one of those dances, though. The headmaster's wife could not seem to keep herself from staring intently at a very beautiful Ethiopian girl as she danced. Her gaze was obsessive and rapt—so much so that she seemed oblivious to anything but the girl. Her mouth hung open and her head jutted forward as if she might fall on her nose. The headmaster averted his eyes and talked politely to someone next to him, and the rest of us pretended not to notice.

In addition to my studies, I was taking ballet classes in Addis Ababa. My Russian teacher would sit on a chair with her feet wide apart and pound a cane up and down on the floor between her legs, calling out, "*Un, deux, trois. Un, deux, trois.*" We would plié and go through the five positions in our ballet slippers. I enjoyed those classes right up until the time we had to leave Ethiopia. "Why did Amy stop her lessons?" the teacher asked my father. "She was good!"

Our six horses were housed in a stable at the top corner of the legation compound, next to the secondary entrance, alongside a chicken farm. Their names were right out of a fornnordic saga: Sleipner, Sirius, Samsoon, and Teal are the ones I remember. They were not exactly Arabic steeds but Ethiopian, and large enough to compete in the local *gymkhanas* and steeple races.

We loved horseback riding, and it was a very social pastime. My mother and father participated in rides around the city, along with many of our Swedish compatriots and American, British, French, and Italian members of Addis Ababa society. Following trails and winding paths through the vegetation and over the hillsides, we would stop and gather for lunch in little glens. Our lunch boxes were delivered by Jeeps and Land Rovers driven to the sites by servants or friends who preferred not to travel to the picnics on horseback.

The first time I was placed in the saddle was on our compound, on the gravel ground that surrounded the house. I was terrified as I felt the strength of the magnificent animal beneath me, and wondered how I could control its motions. As the horse started to trot along, I was instructed on how to use my legs and feet in the stirrups. All went fine until the horse broke into a gallop. *Now what?* At first, I just held on for dear life, but it didn't take me long to get the hang of it and start to enjoy myself.

Many more horseback rides followed, and steeple chases, too, but I did once take a spill. My horse reared and I feel right out of the saddle while one foot remained in the stirrup. I was dragged along for a few seconds, until someone stopped the horse—but what saved me from serious injury was the Ethiopian *chicka,* the very soft mud on the ground. I escaped with nothing more than a sore foot.

We loved our horses and they were a very big part of the Addis social life. The *gymkhanas* and steeple chases were held at a place called Janhoy Meda, where members of the international community would gather dressed in fashions similar to those seen at Ascot racetrack in England.

Then, there were the parties of the diplomatic corps. There were cocktail parties and dinner parties and garden parties and charity events and all of the obligatory visits with new arrivals. Social life there was all about protocol and following strict rules of etiquette. My mother would sometimes complain about the pressure inherent in these formalities—all of the smiling and putting on acts—but it was all part of the scene and necessary to the interest of diplomatic relations among countries.

One day, the emperor came to lunch at our legation. This was an unforgettable event. He was so dignified, and when my mother curtsied for him, he bowed his head. He was accompanied by his entourage of family members, excluding the empress, who suffered from severe diabetes. Both the women and the men were beautiful, with sculpted faces, perfect profiles, and graceful manners. Our Ethiopian servants were delighted to serve their beloved leader. Mammu and Saudi dressed in their best livery and Cookie the cook presided over the kitchen, as usual. Once, when my mother dared to carry a cookbook into Cookie's kitchen, he said, "You read, I know!"

On another occasion, Dag Hammarskjold came to dinner. He was a most distinguished Swede and according to my father, a very hard worker and a lover of poetry, especially that of T.S. Eliot. I remember him standing by the mantelpiece in the drawing room, talking to my father and looking very serious and elegant. Sadly, my father was the one who had to identify him after his tragic death in the suspicious airline crash known as the Ndola incident. Besides Tryggve Lie, he was certainly the finest Secretary-General in the history of the United Nations.

When guests arrived at the legation for dinner or cocktail parties, I would sit on the staircase and watch them all conversing and smoking and drinking martinis. The gentlemen would wear their fine black ties, and the ladies were elegant in their floor-length dresses of brocade, satin, and lamé. They'd drape themselves in fashionably large shawls of various patterns and lots of gold jewelry, especially bangles on their upper arms.

My mother used to say that foreigners were fun to be with, but that "one has the most rewarding times with one's compatriots." In August, our close-knit group of about 500 Swedes enjoyed marvelous crayfish dinners at the legation, an annual tradition. The crayfish was flown in from Sweden and, since

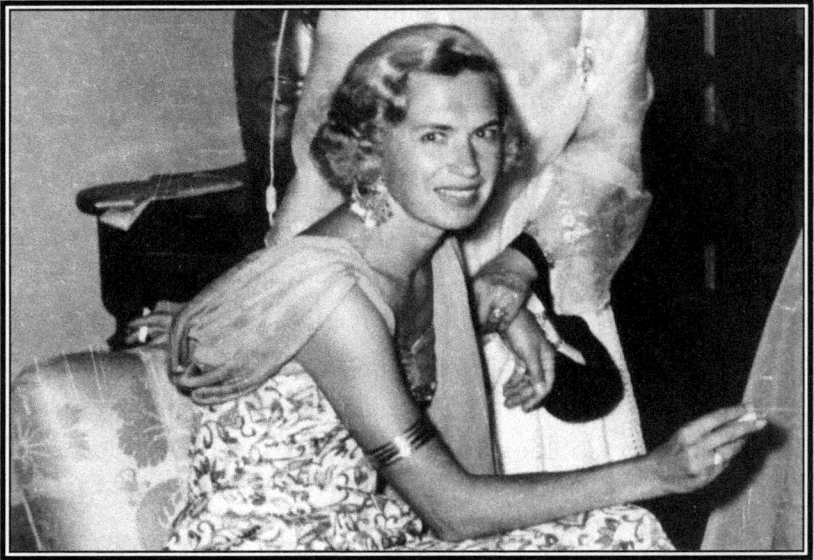

My mother at a party in Addis, 1955.

much schnapps was consumed along with it, many Swedish schnapps songs were sung. We added a special one to the usual repertoire that went, "*Vi tog ett dopp i röda Havet, vi löga där oss minst en kvart, vi trodde vi blev röda av et, men Röda Havet, det blev svart!*" Translation: "We took a dip in the Red Sea, we splashed around for about fifteen minutes, we thought we would become RED, but the Red Sea turned BLACK!" (Because we were so dirty!)

Lucia, or Lady of Light, is another Swedish tradition we observed. On December 13, in the depths of the dark and sinister northern night, Lucia comes to visit and keep the evil spirits at bay. She also delivers comfort to tortured souls. She has candles in her hair, set in a crown of leaves, and wears a long white dress. She is followed by a trail of maidens, all in white with glitter in their hair. Anyone who has seen the procession of Lucia is awed by its beauty, and charmed by the song "Santa Lucia." This is a beloved Swedish tradition, and here we were in Africa, celebrating it just as we would in Sweden. Once, I had the honor of being crowned Lucia, and the real candles on my head dripped into my hair! It took several hours for my friends to help me remove all that wax.

The dance parties were the best. Teenagers of all nationalities would gather in one another's homes and dance the jitterbug, the foxtrot, and even the waltz. There was always Ethiopian music as well. We even had dance competitions. The girls wore stiff petticoats underneath wide skirts, and flat, black ballerina slippers. Our tops were often black off-the-shoulder V-necks. Our hair was set with awful pin curls and combed into weird, stiff-looking do's with bangs. Some of us wore ponytails. We danced into the wee hours, and often fell asleep at five in the morning and stayed overnight. We had such a party at the legation once, but my father let it be known that such overindulgences were forbidden in the future.

"Once Africa, always Africa," the saying goes, but the meaning is hard to explain to anyone who hasn't lived there and experienced it firsthand. The place is a seduction, if you will. It casts a spell with its aromas, its vastness, its Acacia trees, savannahs, mountains, and flamingo lakes, and of course its "bush"— where we ventured in our Land Rovers and Jeeps over stony and perilous paths. But above all, the most fascinating aspect of Africa—or perhaps anywhere—is its animals.

Safaris are wonderful, of course, but when I lived in Ethiopia in the 1950s, it was the animals in the wild, not in the reserves, that made for the deepest enjoyment. We would fill up our vehicles with tents, mosquito nets, and sleeping cots, drive for many hours out of Addis Ababa, and set up camp in the wilderness. The drivers were savvy Swedish gentlemen, experts at changing tires and maneuvering the Jeeps and Land

Rovers around on the winding roads, but sometimes, we would get stuck in the *chicka* or a river and it would take hours to free the cars. Finally, we would arrive at our destination, maybe by a lake or on a clear patch of land, and set up our tents for the night. Remember that this was the 1950s; some of these trips were for the purpose of hunting. But often they were just for pleasure, for enjoying the East African wilderness and its magnificent animals.

The wild game included a variety of antelopes: impala, oryx, bushbok, waterbok, cute little white-bottomed dikdik, rare kudo, and gnu. There were also wild boars with strange-looking snouts. Watching giraffes gnaw at the trees and stride around on their elegant legs was an amazing sight. The pretty zebras with their jaunty behinds ran freely around the open fields. We had to be careful not to get too close to the African crocodiles, which could hide beneath the stones. Someone in our party

Father with a crocodile.

My brother Carl Johan in Ethiopia, 1955.

once sat on a little cliff and barely escaped the sudden attack of one. The hippos and rhinos—what can I say about them? These fleshy, powerful creatures lazed in and by the rivers, to be watched from a distance and admired in awe. To see the magnificent elephants meant venturing much further South, toward the countries of Kenya and Uganda, and were mostly found in the reserves. We made these trips in due time.

The bush trips were such a significant part of our Ethiopian years that it is hard to describe their impact on me. The emotional effect has lasted my entire life. It was the evenings by the campfires I remember most fondly. We were all covered from top to toe to avoid being bitten by the dangerous mosquitos that carried malaria. We sprayed DDT all over the campsite and in our tents, not knowing it was dangerous. (Later, it was banned.). We'd sit around the campfire with our gin-and-tonics, singing Swedish songs such as the one about the Red Sea and many others. It was the most glorious fun in the whole world, and we thought ourselves so very lucky to experience such romance. There, under the dark, star-spangled midnight sky, we could hear the roar of an animal and the barking of hyenas in the distance. The lions of Ethiopia were out there, but we saw one only once—while crossing a river in our Land Rover. It was evening. He stalked across and stared into our headlights for a few moments. What a sight! He seemed a majestic loner, a full-grown male with an impressive mane. Just as quickly as he'd appeared, he disappeared into the night.

My six years in Ethiopia were the most formative of my life, and the experiences of animals in the wild were among my most cherished—and exciting—memories.

One day, the locusts came. Far up in the sky, giant clouds suddenly appeared, maroon-colored, as if a menacing and mysterious thunderstorm were developing. Within an hour, thousands and thousands of the insects descended upon us, and everything green was devoured. Our gardener waved a stick, trying to disperse these ferocious insects, to no avail. We closed all the windows and doors and watched from inside. The effect was like some kind of rainstorm, and in a few hours the locusts were gone. I do not exactly remember what the damage looked like, but the ground must have been barren for quite a while.

Ethiopia has four seasons: a long rainy season and a shorter one, followed by a long dry season and a shorter one. As I recall the wet seasons, the rain would come in subtropical torrents and the vegetation would flourish. The *chicka* would get very thick and the eucalyptus trees grow their beautiful teal-colored leaves. The earth was always red and the trees green, forming the colors of the Ethiopian landscape. At six o'clock in the evening, the darkness would fall like a curtain within minutes, and at six in the morning the light would wake everyone, aided by the crowing of the roosters. At night, we could hear the barking of hyenas all around the city.

The termites were everywhere. Out in the countryside, we saw strange formations of stacked nests in arid areas beside flat-topped acacia trees. This dry landscape could pose a hazard to us bush goers. When we ventured out, we had to take plenty of water as well as gasoline. The canisters took a lot of space in the Jeeps, along with the rest of our equipment.

Even in our elegant home, termites took up residence inside the 1950s lampshades—but they never managed to devour the house. Not that we didn't have structural problems. The wiring in the legation was so badly insulated that taking a bath could result in an electrical shock! Oh yes, that was Africa—but we abided with it all and loved our life.

Then there were the diseases: malaria, hepatitis, amoebic dysentery, tapeworm, biniki worm, as well as plenty of rabies. At twelve years old, I got sick with some form of hepatitis, but it was labeled *jaundice,* which is really just its symptom. I had to stay in bed for about a month with yellowing eyes, and was fed a diet of white meat of chicken and vanilla ice cream, which I did not dislike at all. My mother got amoebic dysentery and was very sick for a while as well. The doctors were very good in Addis Ababa, and thoroughly experienced with tropical diseases. They prescribed penicillin for many things, and it worked very well in those days. Outside Addis was the famous Pasteur Institute, where I had to make several visits, including the time that I had petted a cat that later died from rabies. The injections were administered with huge, thick needles and I had to endure eight of them, at intervals of every other week. They didn't really hurt so much, but my stomach turned into a potato field, we joked, and I walked bent over half the time. On one occasion, the telephone rang in the doctor's office just as he was injecting me. He left the needle in my belly while he answered the call!

We all got booster shots for malaria every six months, and yet it was a common malady. I am happy to say I was spared that one. When my family was still in Berlin, prior to our trip to Ethiopia, we received all the necessary shots for yellow fever, smallpox, and tetanus. Some of these went directly into the chest, next to the heart—and boy, did they hurt! Oh, the 1950s!

I mentioned that Ethiopia was a biblical land, and just as in the Bible, many poor individuals there suffered from leprosy. They begged in the streets, displaying scabs everywhere, their noses and parts of legs and arms falling off. What could one do at that time? A Swedish nurse, a Florence Nightingale kind of woman, had managed to create a special kind of safe house for the children of these unfortunates, in an attempt to protect them from getting infected. She got aid from Sweden, some of which was stolen by the corrupt authorities, but still managed to keep the place functioning. Her positive attitude and strength still amaze me.

A philanthropist named Dr. Edgar Mannheimer led a children's hospital in Addis Ababa that grew into a worldwide health organization. Another doctor, Fride Hylander, was a sort of principal advisor. Having lived in Ethiopia for many years, he was a specialist in all things Ethiopian. It was often frustrating to advise newly arrived, well-meaning Swedish aid workers in how things worked there, and misunderstandings due to cultural differences abounded. "This is the way we do it in Sweden," did not sit well.

We could not drink the water without boiling it, and that included the water we used to brush out teeth. And there was Sinalco, a local beverage similar to Coca-Cola that was popular among Ethiopians. It came in orange or cola flavors.

As I mentioned earlier, our food was prepared by Cookie, supposedly in the French style though it was always a bit "off." We often ate a local dish called *injera wott*—unleavened bread we jokingly compared to "a dirty napkin." We also had artichokes, a variety of chicken dishes, and eggs in berberi sauce, which was very hot, but we got used to it. This was always eaten with one's fingers, by dipping the bread into the dish Cookie would behead the hens behind one of the outhouses on the compound, accompanied by a tremendous amount of screeching and cackling! So much for exotic living.

On March 4, 1955, my little brother was born. We visited my mother at her hospital bed, where she lay with the baby next to her. When we walked in, she was crying! Our beloved shepherd dog Susie had died on that very same day. There was joy and there was sorrow. I was twelve at the time, and emotionally overwhelmed. When we got back home, I threw myself on the doorstep of the house and sobbed.

We never determined the cause of Susie's death, but we suspected she had been poisoned. Another possible cause was an electrical shock due to our poorly insulated wiring. Susie's body was delivered to the Pasteur Institute, though I never really understood why.

Carl Gustaf was the cutest baby you ever saw. "Ladela…. ladela….ladela…." he chirped. At the time, my older brother was at boarding school in Sweden. He would visit us on school holidays, and soon became very familiar with Ethiopia as well.

We had many friends in both the Swedish community and diplomatic society—the British, Americans, French, Italians, German, and, of course the Amharas of Addis Ababa. One British gentleman named Anthony would habitually visit us at lunchtime. He drank gin-and-tonic or Planter's lime juice, and I was in awe of his witty and sardonic way of speaking. I remember particularly that he often used the word "bloody."

There was an Italian aristocrat by the name of Della Ciesa who admired my mother and came around quite often. Mother was very attractive in those days, and she had her suitors. At parties she would wear floor-length brocade, silk, or crepe dresses, accessorized with Ethiopian gold bangles and necklace of all kinds. Her earrings were in the 1950s style, with dangling pearls, and her skin glowed until her suntanning habit started to take its toll.

Some of the Swedes were in the military, and their sons and daughters were my teenage friends. To visit girls named Anna Märta, Per Arne, and Kerstin, among others, we would often travel to Bishoftu, a few miles from Addis, where many of the Swedes lived because it was close to a military base. On that base, local Ethiopians were trained by Swedish instructors to become aviators. One very well-known pilot by the name of Carl Gustav von Rosen had flown in World War II and was a very close friend of my family.

The Swedish engineers who trained the local young men used to say them, "Sooooo, boys, not sooooo!" meaning, "That is the way you do it, not like that." The Swedish accent was very pronounced.

Another thing we joked about was the way the secretary at the legation would answer the phone by calling out, "This is the Sweeedish legation!" We also thought it was funny, when speaking German to someone, to say, "*Das war das das, wie man in Schweden sagen!*" This could be translated as, "That's the end of that!" or simply, "That's that!"

There were scores of diplomatic jokes. Once, when someone arrived at the American Embassy to meet with the ambassador, the "ambassadress" replied in French, "*Mon mari est allé au cabinet avec beaucoup de papiers!*" She'd meant to explain that her husband had gone to the cabinet with many documents, but what she'd said, literally, was, "My husband has gone to the toilet with many paper (rolls)!"

French was spoken just as much as English, because it was (and remains) the language of diplomacy. This has been true since the days of Louis XIV. In any case, French was the principal language all over North Africa, and was spoken by the emperor. English could be heard mainly in Central or South Africa.

In 1955, before my brother was born, we visited Kenya, in Central Africa. In our hotel lobby in Nairobi, I saw guns for the first time in my life. They looked very heavy to me as they hung from the holsters of local British men. These were colonial days, and Mau Mau uprisings were common. We heard many horror stories about the struggles for independence.

We visited Malindi, on the coast of the Indian Ocean, Uganda, and Rwanda Urundi, as it was called at that time. We posed for pictures at the equator. Wherever we went, it was terribly hot and humid and we had mosquito nets over our beds. The British colonials were everywhere, having their afternoon tea and very late evening dinners in formal attire. I remember a meal where shepherd's pie was served, along with plenty of claret and port. I got along well in English, having attended the English school in Addis.

Traveling with our friends the Sandmarks, we visited the Belgian Congo, as it was called then, and saw the pygmys living deep in the jungle. They were very friendly when we greeted them. Mr. Sandmark was a military officer of high rank, and his wife was a spunky and spirited woman, suntanned and good looking. They had three sons who became friends with my older brother when he visited on school holidays. One of the sons, Per Arne, became for a while a kind of beau to me, and, if I remember correctly, gave me my first kiss!

It would all come to an end when I was sixteen. It was 1959, and my father had been appointed ambassador to South Africa. As for me, I had no alternative but to return to Sweden by myself in order to continue my schooling.

Chapter Seven

The Maladjusted Newcomer

1959-1960 SWEDEN

Welcome to "sweet sixteen," the worst year of my life. I arrived in Gothenburg in 1959, and it was decided I should stay with my aunt and uncle at Bäckebol at first; but then, since I had to continue my Swedish education in the city, it seemed best to find lodging for me closer to school. The lady who rented out a room to me, Mrs. Frigård, was kind—but I soon grew uncomfortable in the situation, and ill at ease at the Swedish high school.

I felt like an outcast. To help with my adjustment, I was tutored privately by a very well-meaning gentleman teacher who kept asking me during the lessons, "Why are you in such a hurry?" It was all about nerves and insecurity on my part.

The school was called *Göteborgs Samskola*, and I was admitted into what was known as the First Ring in the four-year Swedish gymnasium. This form of education was roughly equivalent to the French baccalaureate at that time, or two years of American college, depending on one's credits and grades. I know this because my former classmate and best friend, Birgitta, whom I graduated with in Stockholm in 1963, was admitted to the third year of college in Berkeley, California.

This gymnasium is generally considered a secondary academic education. At the time, there were two branches to choose from, the Latin Line and the Science Line. I chose the former, and would study the humanities—i.e., Latin, Greek, history, philosophy, geography, and the European languages. I would complete my education in Stockholm—but I'll get to that later.

So here I was, transplanted to my native country. Rather than a return, it felt as if I had moved to a very strange place where I did not belong. Gothenburg was cold and very windy, situated, as it is, on the west coast of Sweden bordering the Atlantic Ocean. I did make a few friends as I tried to adapt. Connie was a very genuine young lady, if a bit nerdy and frumpy in contrast to Ingrid, who was extremely bright and attractive. She was, however, as the Swedish saying goes, "*Lätt pa foten*"—"light on the foot"—i.e., not so virtuous. Ingrid was always looking for action!

It was 1959 and we all wanted to look like Brigitte Bardot. We would dress up in tight skirts and wide belts and tease our hair into beehives. False eyelashes, thick slanted lines on our upper lids, and pink pouty lips was the look. Thus arrayed, Ingrid and I would trot along to singles bars. Thinking back on it, I can't believe how demeaning it was, sitting on those barstools "waiting" to be picked up for a date, hoping it might turn into a romance. Ingrid enjoyed it; I did not. Coming from Africa, where I had been courted at parties in a more protected environment, I found myself feeling exposed and quite silly. It was all part of the teenage scene, just like everywhere else in the western world. Reluctantly, I'd end up dancing with some young man, eager to give the impression that I was enjoying myself. Some of these boys could be quite rude, I thought, as opposed to the more gentlemanly demeanor of the English, French, and American young men I'd been accustomed to. But perhaps my observations on this should be taken with a grain of salt. I was, after all, a "maladjusted newcomer."

Even after all my years away, I still felt close to Uncle Martin

The maladjusted newcomer (right), 1959.

and Aunt Stina. On my days off from school, I'd go to see them and enjoy their beautiful old house and surrounding grounds. My grandmother had died a few years earlier, and Anna, our beloved housekeeper, had retired to her native Småland. Things are never quite the same as one remembers. The memories of my childhood at Bäckebol will always remain, but at sixteen, I felt that the former magic of the place was gone.

In Gothenburg, I met a distant relative—a cousin to my father—and was completely taken aback by her attitude. She was one of those old-fashioned and rather odd ladies who looked at me sternly. I was not used to that For some reason—I have no idea why—in the midst of a fairly normal

Swedish winter, 1960.

conversation, she blurted out suddenly, "Have you ever seen a naked man?" What was she getting at? I was already feeling maladjusted, and this strange lady seemed to be launching into a weird lecture about sex. Seeing as how I was a virgin at the time, her comment seemed misplaced and bizarre. Perhaps she'd heard about my escapades with Ingrid, but clearly, she had completely misinterpreted them.

As if that were not alienating enough, our conversation about Africa did not go well either. At some point, I made the rather immature but totally innocuous comment that I had grown "tired of elephants." All I meant to say was that we had seen so many of them in Kenya and Uganda that they'd seemed commonplace after a while. That comment did not sit well with her. In a letter to my father, she let it be known that Amy (Aimee) was a very spoiled young lady!

After the naked men and the elephants, I wanted nothing more to do with that particular relative. And she was not the only Bratt family member with whom I had an alienating encounter. Once, many years later, when I was living in the United States, I visited Sweden and attended the yearly Bratt Society meeting, a formal dinner affair. One of the ladies, another cousin of my father's, made some derogatory comment to me, the substance of which I cannot even remember but I know it was rude and tasteless. I think this person felt she could take liberties with me because I had arrived from the U.S. *Just foolish*, I thought, especially since she was a very respected and prominent member of the Bratt Society. In general, the Bratts are a fine family dating back centuries, and I am proud to belong to it.

My boarding situation with Mrs. Frigård proved itself absurd and I did not stay long. She even admitted to me that she preferred to rent to young men, as they did not spend so much time in the bathroom or hang their underwear all over the place! My next best option was to stay with my aunt Ingrid, who also lived in Gothenburg. She was newly married to a man named Bengt, a very nice businessman, and they had an apartment just down the street from Mrs. Frigård. It was a medium-sized apartment—without an extra bedroom—which is probably why I hadn't been sent to them in the beginning.

For a few months the arrangement worked well enough, but over time, my welcome wore thin. Admittedly, it's not easy for a married couple to house a teenager not their own. They tried hard to be tolerant, but I used the telephone constantly, chatting away with my friends even after I had just been with them. And Ingrid and Bengt had their own frictions, as most married couples do. I couldn't deny feeling that I did not belong there.

In fact, my own parents would soon divorce, thus beginning a new phase in my family's life.

Chapter Eight

The French School and the Malaise

1960-1963 STOCKHOLM

It was 1960, and my parents were in South Africa with my little brother, Carl Gustaf. My father was now the Swedish envoy and spent half the year in Pretoria and the other half in Cape Town, where I would soon visit. My older brother, Carl Johan, was in a boarding school in Sigtuna, north of Stockholm. Where was I? In limbo between the two major cities in Sweden.

Stockholm would be my home for the next few years, thanks to my parents' sudden divorce. The reasons for their breakup had something to do with the change of location, but there were other issues, too, none of which are worth going into. In a way, I was somewhat relieved when my father gently broke the news to me, while he was on a short visit to Sweden. I was seventeen years old and thought perhaps it was best, as there had been much tension between my parents in the previous few years. Had the break come earlier—say, when I was twelve and we were still in Ethiopia—it would have been devastating.

My mother came to Stockholm, where she and I and my older brother, who had graduated from boarding school and passed his exams, moved in together. We settled in the suburb called Bromma, on a quiet street in a community called Ålsten. Our very nice house was within a short walking distance to the local tramway, the Blue Line, that went into the center of Stock-holm. Indeed, its cars were very blue. It was all *very boring!*

And then came the *pièce de résistance*. It was decided I should enroll in the prestigious French School. I was admitted into the Second Ring of the Latin Line in order to continue my educa-tion until graduation and the completion of the "student examen," as my brother had done. This elite private girls' school was attended by none other than Princess Christina of Sweden, Antonia Axelson Johnson (heiress to the famous Johnson Ship-ping Line), and the daughter of the opera singer Jussi Björling, among many other girls from prominent Stockholm families. My older brother was dismayed, believing that the school was much too snobbish and possibly overrated. He thought I'd have been better off in a more modest public school. But my father had the final word and, apparently with his influence, I was placed in the Princess's class.

The French School was in a fine old building in the mid-dle of Stockholm, on Döbelnsgatan, next to a church and a park. On its third floor was a French Catholic nunnery; thus the name of the school. We wore blue smocks embroidered with the French Lily near our right shoulders. Once again, I felt "miscast." (I use the term humorously, a habit from my time in New York show business decades later.)

I have an old friend Gunilla, who was then my classmate. She had been asked to try and help me adjust to my new envi-ronment—yet another "edge" for me to "dance around." At first I had a hard time adapting, but as time went by, I devel-oped a few close girlfriends each quite different from one another. There was Gunilla and then Birgitta, who was also a diplomat's daughter. She is the one who later attended Uni-versity of California at Berkeley. And there was Lolo, whose real name was Louise, with whom I spent much time in cafes, smoking and drinking coffee and talking about the world.

Our school was a very good one indeed, with excellent teachers. I was good with languages, and enjoyed my classes in French grammar, reading, and writing; literature; German; and English. Our Swedish teacher, Margareta Tham, was tough! She graded our composition and literature papers quite critically.

Our Latin teacher looked just like the letter I: tall and skinny with a small head like the dot on top. He looked as if he should be wearing a toga, I thought, and, although he was a good teacher, he could be short-tempered when a student didn't answer readily. "If you don't know the answer, at least, *act* as if you do!" he burst out once. He could not stand any sign of insecurity, which gave him little tolerance for seventeen-year-old girls. Though I found him a big pain in the posterior, he did give me a passing grade in Latin. To this day, I remember "Pyramus et Thisbe." We had four hours a week of classes and plenty of homework.

There was a temporary Swedish literature teacher quite good-looking, with a "tough guy" demeanor and a sarcastic tone I'd never before encountered in a teacher. Once, rather tastelessly, he muttered something about making a "Belsen" (referring to the German concentration camp in World War II) out of the class if he got displeased in some way. I think he was a bit perverted!

A wonderful Frenchman taught us French in addition to what we were already learning in our regular curriculum. "*Jeune Fille de Bonne Famille*" he called us, or whatever suited his fancy. He wanted to teach us about the real world, where money was the name of the game. We, protected girls from good families had little to do with that milieu! Clearly, he enjoyed his work, and we enjoyed him. He was a refreshing breeze in the otherwise severe and formal atmosphere of the French School.

There was much drama in the classroom. At our age, we suffered from emotional distress, whether hormonal or the desire for attention, and caused many dramatic scenes, crying and running out of the classroom in teenage despair. Our extreme behavior would have been humorous if it had not felt so real. Our periodic "malaise" was genuine. Keep in mind that this was the early 1960s, and young women were going through phases. Birth control, back-alley abortions…yes, these things touched even privileged girls from "good families." Sweden was not as progressive as it is today, though it was far ahead of the United States in its attitude toward birth control. A decade later, when I lived in the States, I remember shocking a friend of a relative—an American lady—when I mentioned that I had forgotten to take my pill!

Birgitta and I studied together to prepare as best we could for our upcoming exams in Swedish, French, and the rest. The heaps of books we were supposed to read were overwhelming! On breaks, we would walk the Stockholm streets and worry about the future, as young people always do.

With Lolo, we'd frequent the local cafes, ordering coffee and pastries and smoking too many Kent cigarettes—as much as a pack a day! We spoke endlessly about French Cinema—"La Nouvelle Vague"—particularly the films of Truffaut and Goddard. It was about Jean Paul Belmondo, Pascale Petit, and of course Brigitte Bardot, Yves Montand, and Simone Signoret. We railed against the injustices in the world and talked about the existentialism of Jean Paul Sartre. We read his *Huit Clos* (*No Exit*) and Andre Gide's *La Nausée* (*Nausea*)—all the dark post-war philosophy. We obsessed about it, wallowed in it, it was food for our hungry young souls. It was *la malaise*.

I am not sure why we were all so depressed, but this was the atmosphere in Europe in those days. We dressed like stylish

Student examen, with the white hat.

bohemians, in black turtlenecks, tight corduroy skirts, black stockings, and semi-high-heeled shoes with straps. Our hair was teased and our makeup consisted of pink lips and black-lined eyes. I'd carry on this look in Paris a year later, after my graduation in Stockholm.

As the spring of 1963 arrived, our dreaded exams grew near. We faced either great success or great failure. In order to graduate, we'd have to pass written tests as well as oral exams, which would be administered by so-called *censors*, university professors who would arrive on the appointed day. They would ask a few academic questions, and failure to answer them resulted in shame and the repetition of an entire year of the class.

Believe it or not, bad results on these tests resulted in some

Birgitta in New York.

suicides. Ask anyone who went through the experience during the mid-twentieth century. My Swedish uncle, who emigrated to the United States, wrote about it in his memoir.

The good news is that my classmates and I all made it through. Our Swedish teacher, formidable Margareta Tham, had armed us with an interesting and effective way of dealing with the dreaded censors. "Imagine them in *pajamas!*" she'd suggested, and—believe it or not—it worked...for me, anyway. At my impressionable age, it had the effect of a tranquilizer. I don't think it would have made much difference at a more mature time in my life. Today, there is less pressure associated with the "student examen." Those old-fashioned tactics were eventually deemed undemocratic and unfair, for obvious reasons.

Graduation day was celebrated in a big way. We dressed in specially ordered white suits and dresses and purchased the symbolic "white hats"; flower garlands were hung around our shoulders and head; and finally, we were thrown up and down in the air, accompanied by singing and shouting of "hurrah, hurrah, hurrah!" Then, we and our families and friends formed a procession back to our houses, for parties featuring Champagne and lavish food. We celebrated late into the night.

Graduation marked a veritable turning point in our lives. Looking back, I am grateful to have received a fine education at the French School, along with my classmates. During the ensuing years, pictures and stories appeared in the newspapers about graduation day in May of 1963, because of Princess Christina.

Unfortunately, I retained little contact with my former classmates, because I eventually left Sweden for the United States and was hired by Pan American World Airways, as it was called then. My friend Gunilla was hired by Pan Am as well, and has since retired in London. Birgitta went on to interpreting school in Geneva, then worked for the U.N. in

Gunilla in New York.

DANCING AROUND THE EDGE

Pakistan. She has three children and resides in Sweden and France. Lolo lived all over before settling in Sweden, or so I hear. I have lost contact with her. Antonia Axelson Johnson, CEO of the Johnson Line and perhaps the most prominent businesswoman in Sweden, is a good friend of the Princess. Many others became successful in one way or another, including Ann Charlotte Björling (daughter of the opera star), Susanne Ihre, Gabrielle, Annette, Marta, Lena, and the rest. I will always remember them and my Stockholm years.

Chapter Nine

At Sea to Capetown

1961 SOUTH AFRICA

I was seventeen and embarking on a very adventuresome ocean voyage. It was my summer holiday from school and I was going to visit my parents. In those days, people didn't fly very often; we took trains or boats. So, it was arranged for me to travel on a Transatlantic Shipping Line cargo ship from Copenhagen down to South Africa. The boat took only twelve passengers, and it was a very inexpensive way to travel. The journey would take about three weeks, down through the Bay of Biscayne, along the western coast of Europe, then over to Africa and Cape Town, at its southernmost tip.

I boarded the ship in Copenhagen in the early summer of 1961, with one suitcase full of clothes I thought appropriate for Pretoria, where I would be staying with my parents in the Swedish legation. I knew there would be cocktail parties and garden parties, as there had been in Ethiopia, but this would be a different kind of social life—much more colonial. And I knew I'd be witnessing Apartheid, the country's severe policy of segregation and discrimination.

In my book about my father, I wrote about his experiences with the political situation in South Africa, and how he tried to save a black man who had been attempting to flee to Sweden to keep from being arrested. I also wrote about Father's meeting with Verwoerd, the Prime Minister. Father used to refer to the South African Union as "this horrible land."

The twelve passengers on the ship were mainly older couples on vacation. The only other young person that I can recall was the captain's daughter. She was my age and a party girl who loved to drink as much as the sailors did, but we became good friends while on board. She warned me about the wild celebrations when crossing the equator, and sure enough—there would be "baptisms" in water and alcohol! There was this lavish dinner where the centerpiece was a huge hunk of ice that had been frozen around a small replica of the ship, along with lots of flowers. There was plenty of schnapps and the usual singing of schnapps songs.

The ship was a slow one, traveling at a speed of about twelve knots, and when we got to the Bay of Biscayne, the ocean grew very turbulent and stormy. Of course I was seasick, but was promptly given Dramamine, which worked like a dream. Once I felt better, we had a hell of a good time. I could not believe how the captain's daughter could drink! She was very attractive but a bit crazy, and so eager for action that, upon arrival in Cape Town, she got her father's permission to disembark from the ship and accompany me and my father, who met us on the quay, all the way to Pretoria. She was apparently used to traveling all over the world, so this was just another adventure. I think her parents were divorced and her schooling remained a mystery to me.

On board the ship, I had my first real romance. In Ethiopia, I had danced and dated and partied, but just for amusement, shall we say. At sea, the atmosphere was seductive. The horizon, the endless ocean, and the setting sun that looked like yellow jelly disappearing slowly into the sea, were incredibly romantic. My suitor was "Engine Man Number One," for lack of a better title, and he was twenty-four years old and very good-looking. Everybody knew who my father was, so this young man had no intention of making advances that might have seemed inappropriate. What did we do? We just sat on a bench watching the setting sun and holding hands. That was it. It was all very innocent.

At the end of the journey, as we approached Cape Town, I knew this "romance" had to end, and I was quite sad and reluctant to leave the ship. He, too, looked a little disappointed—and quite surprised when, as the ship anchored in the harbor, my father was there to meet me, along with a local newspaper crew who took pictures and wrote a story about my arrival. The next day, a very windblown picture of me would appear in the paper, along with a few corny lines about my school exams, written in Afrikaans.

I will never forget my father standing there, at first all alone in the early evening, waving his hands back and forth and calling out, "Amy! Amy!!" I was a bit embarrassed by that grand display of emotion, but long family separations are common in the diplomatic world, and there is genuine happiness when meeting again. I remember one point in my life when my father was in Teheran, my mother in Sweden, my brothers somewhere else in Europe, and I in the United States.

I disembarked with the captain's daughter, and my father did not mind her presence at all. The three of us proceeded to take a short sightseeing tour of beautiful vintage Cape Town, surrounded by mountains.

We traveled by car all through Bloomfontein to Pretoria. The countryside was a feast for the eyes. Eventually, we came upon the famous Kruger National Park. In Ethiopia, wild animals had been difficult to spot, but not so in Kruger. We saw lions lazing in their lairs and zebras and other wild game all around—abundant. But most majestic of all were the elephants.

"Elephants have right of way," read the humorous British signs displayed here and there.

I had seen the reserves in Kenya and Uganda of course, and it was quite similar here. In those days, we never heard anything about poaching. There were safaris, but they were far less common and commercial than they are today. I worry now, when I hear about visitors getting too close to the animals and making too much noise. It is so important for the wildlife that we keep our distance and respect nature.

Finally, we arrived in Pretoria and it was time for the captain's daughter to bid us farewell. Eventually, her father notified us that she had to return to the ship—to go back to Scandinavia, I believe.

My mother greeted us at the door of the residence which was located in an area called Constantia, slightly outside the city. My little brother, five at the time, was attending kindergarten there, and not present upon our arrival. The house was beautiful, with a large garden, but mostly what I remember is the living room, which had a fireplace surrounded by comfortable sofas and armchairs.

Soon, I was introduced to Pretoria social life. There were far fewer Swedes there than had been in Ethiopia, and mostly I met British and Boers—former Dutch—whose first language was Afrikaans. They lived in opulent villas with surrounding grounds and behaved very much like the original colonials, with their uppity mannerisms and upper-class disregard for anyone who voiced opposing opinions about Apartheid. "For goodness sake, don't talk about politics here!" was the general warning.

Local native servants cooked, cleaned, took out the garbage, and mowed lawns for very little pay, if any. The British

Mrs. Eyvind Bratt, wife of the Swedish Minister, with her daughter, Amy, at a cocktail party which Dr. and Mrs. Bratt gave at the Swedish Legation last week. Amy, who is spending her school vacation in the Union, will return to Sweden at the end of the month, accompanied by her mother. Mrs. Bratt will return to South Africa to join her husband in Cape Town for the next Parliamentary session.

Newspaper clipping showing my mother and me at a Swedish Legation cocktail party.

were perhaps a tad more humane than the Boers in their treatment of the local population, but Apartheid had created an awful and senseless situation. Non-whites were expected to carry special passports for identification, and could be stopped at any time by the police. If they could not produce this document right away, they were arrested.

When picking up my father from an appointment, our chauffeur, Jacob, had to use a different elevator for "colored people," leaving my father to wonder where he'd wandered off to. Once, Jacob took my mother and me to visit his house in one of the "ghettos." It was actually quite orderly and well maintained, considering the poverty and oppression he and his people were living with.

Among the privileged, it was all about parties. There were horse steeple races and *gymkhanas*, along with opulent garden parties, black-tie dinners, and cocktail events within the diplomatic community. The younger set with whom I became acquainted had many dancing events. Besides American rock 'n' roll and jazz, I was introduced to the famous African "kwela." Oh what a sound: rhythmic like ocean waves, slow and seductive and very unique. The dance steps moved back and forth, up and down with the rhythm. I was given a record of the most popular tunes and cherished it, hoping to dance to it again in Stockholm. Later, back at the French School, I placed it in my classroom desk for a few days and—can you believe it?—someone stole it!! What a sordid thing to do, especially in a prestigious school like that one. We had few outsiders on the premises…was it one of my classmates?

My stay in Pretoria lasted the full three months of my holiday from school. I have no recollection of my trip back to "boring" Stockholm, but it certainly wasn't on a transatlantic ship.

It was in the fall of 1961 when, on a short visit to Stockholm, my father and I took a walk around our neighborhood in Bromma and he told me about the divorce. As I said earlier, I really didn't think it was such a bad idea. I was almost eighteen and understood very well that such a separation could be in the best interest of all.

My mother, however, would have a hard time adjusting to losing her status as a diplomat's wife and the comfortable life that went with it. She would have to get used to living in a more ordinary way, and was not prepared for it at all. I want to mention this only in passing, and not go further into it—but I feel I must explain that it was my mother who might be assigned blame for the breakup—not my father, who loved her very much!

Stockholm was so cold in the winter, often getting down to twenty-below Celsius (minus-five Fahrenheit). At seven in the morning I had to stand outside and wait for the Blue Line tramway to take me into Stockholm, then travel by subway to school. I was a naturally late sleeper, and could never get used to those early-morning hours. I never got enough sleep as a teenager, and suffered through the endless hours of class time yawning and feeling miserable, but somehow managing to get good grades. I was mainly motivated by fear of failing all those tests, so I studied diligently, along with my best friend Birgitta.

Birgitta's father was also a well-known diplomat, by the name of Per Anger. He had worked in Budapest with Raoul Wallenberg, the courageous and humane man who saved thousands of Jews from being deported to concentration camps during World War II. Wallenberg gave Swedish passports to many Hungarian Jews so they could flee to Sweden, which was a neutral country. As is well known, he was eventually nabbed by the Russians in Budapest and never heard from again. The Swedish government tried for many years to get answers from the Russians regarding his disappearance but never succeeded. Some felt they did not try hard enough. The tragic fate of this hero is the subject of many books, including one by Per Anger.

Birgitta and I will always have the special bond that forms between certain friends. Later in our lives, we'd meet in New York from time to time, having discovered mutual friends along the way in Sweden, Paris, and the U.S. My other friend,

Gunilla, who was hired by Pan-Am shortly after I was, lived in the U.S. for a while and finally settled in London.

My Stockholm years would soon come to an end, and Paris was on the horizon. Many who attended the French School continued their educations in France and became fluent in the language. That is exactly what I did, not exactly knowing what awaited me.

In the summer of 1963, after my graduation in May, I had a few jobs, including selling postcards to American tourists at the Stockholm Town Hall, a beautiful building by the river with a golden crown. While doing that, I met an American student with whom I went on a kind of date. I was curious about New York, having had a certain premonition about it, so I asked him what it was like. "It's BIG!" he responded. This was NOT very helpful! When he came to pick me up for dinner, he showed up in sneakers! That was the end of that rendez-vous!

One of the few good things about living in Stockholm at that time was my jazz ballet classes. I loved the drums and the black leotards and the electric dancing. The drummers were always African-American and the teachers from New York or Chicago. I was a good dancer, and was placed in the front line every time. The rhythms reminded me of the musical *West Side Story*. I danced in those classes for all of my years in Stockholm.

In the fall of 1963, I took the train to Paris.

Chapter Ten

Mannequin on Rue St. Honoré

1963-1964 PARIS

I arrived in Paris in 1963, at the Gare du Nord train station. It was October and I was about to turn twenty. In those days, it was expected of young Swedish girls that they find jobs and become independent, while continuing with their studies as best as they could. I did not care about furthering my education at the time; I just wanted to get out of Sweden, where I felt oppressed, and go to Paris. Nearly all of my fellow graduates of the French School ventured off to France, England, or Switzerland, including Princess Christina.

Certain other students arriving in Paris enrolled in the Alliance Française, which was for people who had no background in French. This institution was looked down upon as "below par" by many snobbish French people. In any case, I was less interested in studying than in having fun! Paris at that time was a kind of Mecca for young people; the epicenter of European culture, the avant-garde, and art of all kinds. It was filled with cafes, restaurants, fashionable boutiques, and *boîtes de nuits*—nightclubs.

Suitcase in hand, I trotted along by myself until I found a little hotel called Hotel du Parc, located in a small rotunda on the Rive Gauche, not far from the train station. There were little shops lining the side streets nearby, filled with tempting fashion items and seductive French lingerie. There were also bistros that served *café au lait* and *café crème* with magnificent croissants in the morning, and *sandwich au jambon* and *les oeufs en gelée* for lunch. The hotel was very inexpensive and the proprietor was a very kind and helpful, slightly corpulent Frenchman. I secured a perfect little room, then ventured out to see the sights.

Very soon, I grew accustomed to frequenting the famous cafes along the Left Bank. There was La Coupole, La Rotonde, Le Select and Les Deux Magots, where Jean Paul Sartre once sat with his literary entourage and Ernest Hemingway wrote *A Moveable Feast*. The atmosphere evoked the Lost Generation after World War II: Gertrude Stein and Alice B. Toklas. The students talked endlessly about Existentialism, a literary-philosophic cult of nihilism and pessimism that was in vogue in France after the war. It maintained that our very existence in the universe was purposeless. The only way to thrive in this hostile environment was through the exercise of free will. This philosophy resonated with me, after the malaise I had experienced in Sweden. It appealed to my sense of imagination and emotional frame of mind.

It was all so very literary and profound. And in addition to all of my musings, I learned to speak French fluently. I acquired *des petits amis* (little friends) in those cafes, and every day I would arrive in a perfectly Parisian outfit I'd bought in one of the little shops and join my friends—mostly foreign students from the Middle East—to sip Muscadet wine. Aside from Sartre, our conversations were always about romance and politics, specifically the doings of General de Gaulle.

The French are very analytical and opinionated and yes, chauvinistic. In conversation, they usually wanted the last word—and insisted they were right. If you contradicted them, you soon found yourself in a no-win situation. Having said that, I did learn to speak Franch very quickly.

The food was the best I'd ever had. In La Rotonde and La Coupole, it was *les moules* (mussels), *les escargots* (snails), *le biftek* (steak), and *les pommes frites*, the last thin and tasty, with sauce Bearnaise. There was *la choucroute* and *soupe* à l'*onion* at Les Halles, a restaurant further south within the city, and the vegetable dish, *la ratatouille*. Some restaurants served *la fondue au fromage* (cheese fondue), and then there were the magnificent creperies. Some of them were close to my hotel, inexpensive, and very tempting. Crepes were also sold on the street and it was difficult to pass them by without buying one. Paris was the only place in this world where I actually gained weight! Ironically, it is also where I landed my job as *mannequin* (model) in one of the fashion houses on Rue St. Honoré.

I did not intend to stay at Hotel du Parc for longer than necessary, and soon an opportunity to move came along. My mother sent me a letter in which she mentioned a Hungarian couple, friends of my parents from Stockholm, who knew of a young German journalist, Marlet Shaake, who resided in Paris and needed a roommate. She lived on Rue Soufflot, on the Left Bank, and I contacted her.

Marlet turned out to be a very accomplished writer for the *Paris Gazette*. She was twenty-four but behaved more like someone in her forties, and reminded me of Simone Signoret. She immediately accommodated me in her rather large apartment, where I would sleep on a sofa, which was good enough for me at that time. I gathered my belongings from the hotel and moved right in.

It was November 1963. A few days before I left the Hotel du Parc, as I entered the lobby, I glanced at the newspaper on proprietor's desk. The headline read, "Kennedy Assasiné." It

Mannequin 1964: "The Look."

was surreal. At the time, we were not used to these kinds of violent happenings in the world. I think most people remember where they were on that terrible day. The whole world paused for a moment to mourn the loss of the young and beloved American president. Parisians cried in the streets, not just for him but for his wife Jacqueline, whose father was of French extraction. It took a long time for this sad news to settle in people's minds, especially in Europe, where Kennedy had represented the freedom and prosperity of the United States after the devastating war.

At Rue Soufflot, I met several of Marlet's friends. There was Tommy, a sort of bohemian young German radical type who made sarcastically humorous comments about politics. Marlet also had a bunch of American friends who frequented a popular American bar.

We had little parties on Rue Soufflot, and at one of them, someone mentioned to me that I should try modeling. She went on to tell me about a very good modeling school on the Right Bank, next to the Eiffel tower. I got intrigued and decided to check it out.

I don't remember what street it was on, but I walked over to the school—the Ecole de Mannequins—and was accepted right away. Two Parisian ladies ran it. One of them could be described as *la Parisienne:* very slim, elegant, and sophisticated, with glossy raven hair and graceful mannerisms. The other was her *petite amie:* heavy-set, brusque, and mannered.

Modeling lessons were held every day. Back and forth we would walk, one foot in front of the other, our bodies held absolutely still and tilted slightly backwards. The look was *pas de ventre, pas de fesse*, no belly, no behind. . . all very flat and straight, the bust small. We were trained in how to carry *le sac* (purse), *le manteau* (coat), *la parapluie* (umbrella), all while executing the perfect walk and turn. We were taught a variety of ways to wrap a shawl around our shoulders, including what was called *"Le Van Dongen"* after a Dutch artist who painted huge wraps of shiny satin tied around ladies of the nineteenth century. I think we must have learned at least twelve versions of shawl-wrapping and -tying.

"*Ques-que c'est, cette espèce de peruque?!*" exclaimed Madame one day, pointing to my dyed hair. Another time she said, "*Mais, evidement, les hommes vous regarde!*" ("No wonder the men look at you!"). She felt I wiggled too much when I walked in the street. The model walk was a very disciplined style at the time—a far cry from today's strutting down catwalks to blaring rock music.

Aside from teaching the modeling basics the school served as an agency, which was really the whole idea of attending it. When I got my first modeling call, I was told to walk over to a Maison de Coutûre on Rue St. Honoré. It was made clear to me that you weren't guaranteed the job. "*Si vous plaisez!*" they bluntly declared: "If they *like* you!"

Barbara, the first "madame" I was to meet, liked me enough that I was hired. The fashion house was called Ferrara, and was managed by a very gentle, velvet-eyed Italian man in his forties named Antonio Ferrara. He had bought and taken over the house from a more famous Parisian designer named Charlotte Appert. It was situated in the middle of Rue St. Honoré right next to the Boulevard St. Honoré where the big fashion houses were. There was Dior (before Yves St. Laurent), and Coco Chanel was making her famous suits just up the street. There were the houses of Givenchy, Balmain, and Balenciaga in the other direction. The *mannequins* in these houses were all beautiful and very slim, but they were working more for prestige than money; they were paid only a thousand francs per month (about $160.00). I, on the other hand, was about to make 600 francs a month, because Ferrara was not so famous.

Up one flight of stairs was a room where important women sat at their desks. Madame Moulin, a very dainty and exquisite French woman of the old world, spoke rapidly and deliberately. Her comments were critical. The seams and cut of every suit had to be perfect. Another important woman, whose name I can't remember, was just the opposite of Mme. Moulin. She reminded me of an angry bulldog, short, with a large face and a flat little body. "*Il me faut rien, il me faut rien!*" she'd growl. (I must have nothing!) She was referring to her own distinctive way of dressing, which was quite plain. Mainly, she'd wear simple sheaths with zero decorations, no pleats—*rien*! She was very temperamental and would grimace when she spoke; it was fascinating to watch.

Barbara, by contrast, was very nice. "*C'est a cause de moi que tu es ici!*" she'd remind me. ("You are here because of me!") She was often on a diet, prompting the slim Mme. Moulin to ask, "*Barbara, vous êtes aux carottes maintenant?*" in a patronizing tone. Are you into carrots now?

The seamstresses toiled away in a very stuffy back room, pressured by the impending deadline for completion of "*La Collection,*" which was to be modeled by me and a model named Emilie.

I heard that the seamstresses were often not paid on time, and sometimes not at all! We models, on the other hand, were always paid quickly and in cash because we were "*les mannequins de la maison!*"

A wonderful French girl named Nicole made all of the illustrations of the garments. She was excellent, but she, too, had to struggle to get paid. I suppose Ferrara had a hard time making money, as the house was small and its customers few. He made beautiful clothes, though, and I was given a few stunning outfits. One especially beautiful emerald green suit was in my wardrobe for many years.

Now we come to Emilie, the other model. *Mon dieu, quelle Parisienne!* She was twenty-seven years old when I met her and already divorced, which was quite unusual for a Frenchwoman in those days. "*Tu ne comprends pas!*" she'd snap—"You don't understand!"—not even trying to explain the difficult legal aspects of her divorce. I was not very interested anyway. A divorce in France at that time must have been very hard on a woman. Emilie had one son. One day, as we sat in her apartment on the Right Bank, near the Eiffel Tower, she suddenly slapped her little boy across the face—just for something he said. "*Tais toi!*" she spat. ("Shut up!") French parents can be very strict, not unlike the teachers at the European schools of the era.

Emilie was very good-looking of course, with red hair and an excellent figure. "*J'ai beaucoup de succes sur la plage!*" she boasted one day. ("I have MUCH success on the beach!") The beach she referred to was the Riviera.

This is how our days went. We would arrive at ten o'clock in the morning and sit around in a special room waiting to be fitted. The clothes were measured and sewn right on our bodies, so that they would fit perfectly. There was a tremendous amount of fussing about seams and the cut and everything that goes into the creation of a designer look. There were endless discussions about the clothes. When Mme. Moulin thought the result less than perfect, she'd shout, "*Mais alors, il faut que ca soit jolie!*" ("But it has to look beautiful!")

Like the rest of Paris, we had a two-hour break for lunch, which usually consisted of a sandwich and red wine. At around two pm, we would model the collection of suits, dresses, and coats for the customers. Emilie and I would change into the various outfits, then parade back forth using that special walk we'd learned. I remember a few American customers who looked quite bewildered and out of place in this very Parisian environment—but they did end up buying a few items.

When the day was over I'd take the metro back to the Rue Soufflot, where we'd spend many evenings drinking yet more red wine and smoking Gitanes or Gauloises. When I decided that the French cigarettes were too strong for me, I switched to Kents—but still consumed a pack a day!

Marlet was a mature woman and our conversations were full of advice from her. One evening she made a most significant comment: "You should become a Pan Am stewardess!" Never could I have imagined that this would come true.

It's important to understand that a career as flight hostess, as they were called at the time, was considered a major success, especially at one of the prestigious international airlines: Pan Am, TWA, SAS, Air France, BOAC, Lufthansa, or KLM. Fluency in several languages was a requirement, as was a college-level education. The competition was fierce, and very few of the thousands of applicants made the cut.

In those days, it was not just a job, it was a lifestyle—and everybody knew it. It meant flying all over the world, with layovers in exotic places that lasted several days. This was the kind of time off that no other job could offer; it was the opposite of nine-to-five, and that really appealed to me. I was not so sure I would qualify, but when Marlet mentioned Pan American, I sensed something. I was used to Americans and their ways, and this airline would be my first choice, unquestionably.

I filed the idea away in my brain, because, at that moment, I had other fish to fry. The summer was coming up and I very much wanted to visit the Riviera. In one of the Left Bank

Cafes, I'd met a German girl named Karin who sold German fashions. She had had a disastrous affair with a Moroccan student, become pregnant, and suffered the ordeal of a back-alley abortion. Much later, she met an American who we'll call Jim, from New Jersey. Jim was going to arrange a pension in the south of France, and Karin and I decided to take the train down with him to visit Menton, Nice, and Cannes. We thought of it as a summer adventure. Before we left, I moved in with her in Porte de Versailles, ending my time on Rue Soufflot with Marlet. Karin's apartment would be my third domicile in one very formative year in Paris.

Working at Ferrara had been a valuable experience, but I decided to leave that as well, and also to say goodbye to an on-and-off boyfriend named Michel. He'd never been that interesting to me really, just someone to go out with. There had been others, too, including a warm-hearted and amusing older man with whom I had no romance, and a very good-looking Iranian with whom I had a fling for only one night.

Karin's little apartment in Porte de Versailles was a long subway ride from the center of Paris and it was very spartan, without even a refrigerator. "We have to have one," I told her, but she simply didn't feel it was necessary. She'd grown up in Berlin during the war, and considered a fridge a luxury. We had a lot of fun together, but got into numerous arguments based on the characteristic stubbornness of both the Germans and the Swedes. "You attack!" she would say. Could be!!

One evening, we were out on the town with two dates, about whom I can remember nothing except that they took us to various nightclubs where we danced to jazz. Then came what they insisted would be the highlight of the evening. They took us to a dark little place where we witnessed some prostitutes performing a voyeuristic show, mainly for the gentlemen. It was so ridiculous! These poor women performed listlessly with a variety of sex toys…pretty ho-hum, if you ask me. "We can DO much better than that, can't we?" commented one of them afterwards. But it was almost morning and we did not DO anything! Goodbye!

Karin, Jim, and I arrived at the Riviera as planned. Our time there remains a rather memorable experience, one of the oddest in my life, and Jim from New Jersey was the reason for that.

I asked Jim what he did for a living. Cryptically, he answered, "I am looking for a little old lady to inherit from." He turned out to be a con artist. These types weren't usual in Europe—or, not that we knew of—so we really didn't understand what we were in for. One evening Jim gave us hashish. Drugs were certainly new to me so I was cautious, but Karin got very high. Jim was quite taken with her, and just lay back on the sofa, watching as she moved around the room, rambling and behaving strangely from the drug. So this was how our Jim was making his money; he was dealing drugs, doing business with traffickers in North Africa, Morocco, and Tunisia. I also heard about white women were being kidnapped and sold into slavery in North Africa!

In spite of Jim and his shadiness, we managed to have a wonderful time in the sun. We took boat rides on the Cote d'Azur and had dinners of the thin sliced pizza in the city of Nizza (Nice), along with plenty of white wine. I had couscous—an Arabic buckwheat dish—for the first time. I danced in night clubs and jazz clubs and attended performances by immensely popular American artists, including Ray Charles. I developed quite a tan— the darkest I have ever had. "*Vous êtes brune!*" commented one of my dates. Karin and I wore our bikinis with pride.

Karin confided in me that Jim did not know how to kiss. *Il embrace drôlement!"* was how she put it. The affair ended abruptly and he went back to New Jersey. *"Quel salop,"* Karin would say about him later, in letters to me in Sweden. "What a jerk!"

The summer of 1964 was coming to an end and it was time for me to start thinking seriously about my future. I was summoned back to Stockholm, where my older brother had come up with an idea about what I should do. He thought I should go to Schartau, a commercial college, to learn about advertising, distribution, commercial law, and such things. *How boring,* I thought, but I knew he sometimes had good ideas, and advertising was a hot new field.

So, in the fall of 1964, I was admitted into this school in Stockholm. I was twenty-one years old and that was the year I "matured," as my mother put it. She felt that I had finally learned to speak up for myself. Unlike today's young people, my generation of girls tended to be a bit inhibited when growing up. That changed quickly!

Chapter Eleven

Brotherly Advice –Schartau

1964-1965 STOCKHOLM

Back in Stockholm, I now lived with my mother on Nyod-lingsvägen in Ålsten, a suburb of Bromma. My older brother, Carol Johan, was there also, studying at the university. He had a lot of friends who had all gotten married rather young, as did he, to a girl named Birgitta Sandin. We called her Birdie, a nickname her father had picked up on business trips to the United States. She became a very close family friend throughout the ensuing years. I remember her sitting by our fireplace in a chic navy-blue dress. She was attractive and reminded us of Linda Evans. Like most Swedish girls, she was very well educated and held several jobs. Birdie and Carl Johan eventually had two sons, Gustaf and Carl Fredrik.

My younger brother, Carl Gustaf, was nine at the time, and going to school in the neighborhood. As I mentioned earlier, he had been born in Ethiopia and spent the early years of his schooling there and in South Africa. Although he'd lived with my parents all that time, he'd been unaware of any frictions between them. Those wonderful years in Ethiopia had masked the discord between my parents, but their marriage was bound to end up as it did. I am happy to say that they always remained friends and exhibited mutual respect—in part because of their shared sense of humor. The bond between them was never really severed, and they would end up remarrying each other some years later.

At this time, however, my father was the Swedish Envoy in South Africa, and had met and married to someone else. She was an English lady by the name of Sondra, and she would accompany him to Teheran—his new post—in the mid-sixties. We children were in frequent contact with our father, and my younger brother and I would visit him in Teheran in 1965-66.

I was twenty-one years old when I was admitted into the commercial institute called Schartau, and I found myself struggling with the curriculum. There were courses in Swedish and English business language; mathematics, at which I did not excel; bookkeeping and distribution; administration and organization; commercial law; social economics; and typing. The purpose of the course of study was to prepare students for jobs in marketing and distribution, as well as in advertising, which was the hot new field for young people at the time. My class consisted of twenty-six young men and four young women. You can imagine that this was a bit challenging for me, but I am grateful that my brother recommended it, because it had a kind of maturing effect, as my mother would note. For the most part, the teachers were not very inspiring; one of them even told us quite calmly how very boring he was. However boring he might have been, he did win an award of some kind for inventing the little dash over the T in the name Westinghouse! He reminded me of my Latin teacher from the French School who'd looked like the letter I, long and thin with a head like a dot.

I attended Schartau for two semesters and got my diploma, though my grades were just average. My forté remained languages, not economics, but the degree did help me land a few jobs. The course I'd taken in advertising yielded a most interesting job as a field interviewer, calling people on the phone and asking them about their choices of detergents and so forth. This

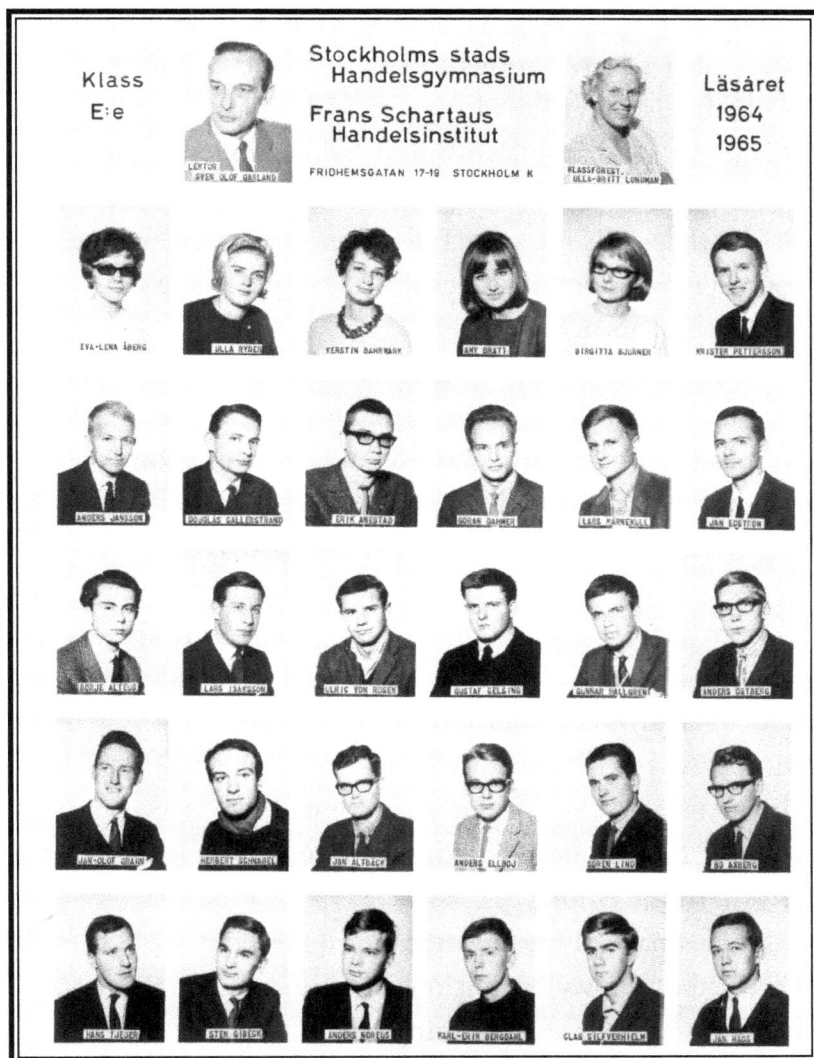

My Schartau class; only five girls among the guys.

was not telemarketing as it is today, but much more personal. Since I had a good voice, my customers tended to respond politely. It was great fun, and the first "real" job I'd ever had.

I soon found myself becoming a businesswoman, traveling by train all over Sweden and making appointments with people for marketing interviews. I also had a job in the Stockholm archives office, where I typed letters and kept administrative order. Each of my various jobs lasted a few months, and I simultaneously continued my jazz ballet classes at least twice a week. Most of my friends and fellow students conducted their lives as I did, traveling, working, and studying all at once. Perhaps it is the same today, but it may have been easier for us to move around, especially in Europe, where train travel was easy and affordable.

I had developed a few new friends during my time at Schartau, but these relationships were short-lived because I was soon ready to desert my native country once again. As I had previously when in Sweden, I was feeling that odd, oppressive malaise again as I flew over my native country. The view was of endless forests of pine trees, and of a faint bluish light that seems to blanket everything. I don't know why this is, but it has always sent my mood into a blue stage. For me, Sweden has always conferred a strange melancholy. When you arrive at Arlanda Airport, where—unlike the bustling terminals everywhere else—there is no noise. There is a law against excessive airport noise in Scandinavia, as it is considered harmful to the employees.

Swedes have always been rather quiet, and are not easily impressed by showy expressions of temperament or emotion. They tend to scoff at such things. I am told that Sweden has changed, perhaps because of the influence of immigrants, but that blue light still envelops one's body and soul. The short days and long dark nights of winter have an effect; a kind of heaviness and melancholy settle in on a daily basis.

It's no surprise, then, that Swedes love to travel, particularly to places filled with sun and warmth and exoticism— parts of the U.S., or Spain, Italy, and France, where many have second homes.

Although I felt oppressed in my native country, I want to point out that Sweden is one of the most advanced countries in the world—and not "socialistic," as it is sometimes misunderstood to be, especially in the States. In fact, it has a multi-party system. Although taxes are admittedly high, it is a good country with wonderful traditions, such as Christmas, Lucia feasts, crayfish parties in August, and more. There is little wrong with Sweden, and I would defend it and my fellow countrymen any time.

Having said all that, I was now ready for new adventures. It was time to act on my abiding interest in Pan Am, so, on December 4, 1965, I went up to the Grand Hotel by the beautiful Stockholm quay for the famous interview. I was about to enter a new phase of my life, but before that, I was on my way to Teheran, accompanied by my little brother.

Chapter Twelve

Pearl Grey Caviar

1965 TEHERAN

A s we had not seen our father in a while, it seemed like a good idea to spend Christmas with him. But first, I'd have to get through my Pan Am interview.

I've already written a book about my Pan Am experiences, called *Glamour and Turbulence,* which starts with a description of the interview process. I won't go into it in depth here; I'll just say that I did very well because I spoke English fluently and didn't mind having my appearance scrutinized and my walk checked. As we all understood at that time, our looks and personality were important, as well as our fluency in languages and a college-level education. We were expected to be attractive, outgoing, and confident. Our height had to be between five-foot-three and five-foot-six; we could weigh no more than 130 pounds; and we had to have 20/20 vision in both eyes.

In the course of our interviews, our skin, hair, and figure were closely judged. Did this make Pan Am discriminatory? Perhaps, but they were no different from any other airline in this regard. That's the way it was in the mid-sixties. As I said earlier, these were high-prestige jobs for women—glamour jobs. Hundreds of eager applicants were screened the same day I was.

At the end of my interview, I was one of the few who was asked to come back that afternoon for a second meeting. I figured it was my easy way of communicating in English that had given me an edge. The second round went well also, and I was asked to bring a little present to a Pan Am representative in Teheran—a good sign, I thought. (Knowing that Teheran was a major destination for the airline, I'd told them about my impending trip.)

I wasn't told whether I would be hired by Pan Am I'd have to wait to find out. "We'll let you know by letter," they told me. I thanked them and departed with the little gift I was to deliver.

I would wait for that Pan Am letter for an agonizing four months. Why was it so important to me? Simply because there was no other job in the world—no other lifestyle—that I wanted so badly.

Carl Gustaf and I boarded the SAS flight for Teheran and, a few hours later, were met happily by our father and driven by his chauffeur to the Swedish embassy residence. It was there that we met Sondra and some high drama began.

My father's second wife was a British colonial type. She was attractive and very poised, in her forties—possibly a good image of an ambassador's wife. Her manner was deliberate and measured, and she was quite engaging to talk to, but almost immediately I noted ominous signs of possessiveness toward my father. She addressed my ten-year-old brother as "Master" Carl Gustaf, as was the custom in upper-class British society, and said she was looking forward to having my assistance in the running of the house. What wishful thinking! I had no intention of acting the cooperative stepdaughter. I wanted to enjoy the diplomatic social life of Teheran as I waited for the all-important Pan Am letter.

This was during the reign of the Shah and Iran, was very friendly with the West. In my book, *Diplomat, Poet, Gentleman: My Father* I describe his meeting with the Shah, whom he found to be a very dignified monarch. I'll repeat only one

significant remark the Shah made. He said he was very worried about the neighboring Arab countries such as Iraq, and
the rise of "Arab nationalism." The future would prove his
concern very well-founded. At the time that I visited, well
before the revolution that would change everything, the Shah
reigned supreme and Iran resembled many European countries, culturally and socially. His wife, Farah Diba, was an
exquisite lady, admired all over the world. She was French-ed-
ucated, spoke several languages, and wore the most beautiful
fashions of the time. She had that sixties look: teased-up bee-
hive hairdo, black eyeliner, and expensive jewelry. She was not
snobbish at all—on the contrary—she was very gentle, and
this added to her popularity and respect. The Shah had a large
family, and it seemed that at every party I attended, I'd meet
some nephew or other relative of his.

Carl Gustaf and I settled in at the residence, which was
rather typical of embassy homes, with fine furniture, but a bit
more posh than the ones in Africa had been. Teheran was a
prominent post for a Swedish envoy, as it was a strategic center in the Middle East. It was also close to Moscow, which was
a post my father had always wanted, as he spoke Russian and
had gathered a lot of knowledge about the region from his
diplomatic experiences in the Baltic states. He was very close
to getting it until Sondra's disastrous behavior had a negative
impact. "She ruined my career," he'd proclaim later.

Father was a formidable diplomat, a Doctor of Philosophy, and the author of several books and articles. He spoke
seven languages and received many medals for his services and
achievements. He was also a prolific poet. There is no question that he was a very accomplished man.

The day after our arrival in Teheran, I became ill. A Dr.
Amiri was summoned and he soon became a good friend and

Swedish emblem on the embassy entrance.

integral part of our social life. I felt better in plenty of time to celebrate Christmas Eve with my family. Presents were doled out and Christmas dinner served, accompanied by lots of conversation during which I was introduced to Sondra's personality. She did her best to be charming but, as I noted, I spotted cracks in her careful façade.

On Christmas Day, after a stroll around the town, we returned to the residence of a proper English supper. I believe it included Shepherd's Pie, Stilton cheese, and port wine. Sondra was the perfect hostess.

On December 26, we were invited to a black-tie dinner at the home of the Posettes, my father's closest secretary at the Embassy and his rather flamboyant but very pleasant Swedish wife. Sondra, who didn't like competition, would soon take issue with her. According to my diary, by December 27, she'd begun acting up and making scenes. I can't recall what it was, specifically, that had upset her, but she grew obsessive and overly possessive of my father. She would voice objections to every little thing. For example, once when we were having

English-style afternoon tea—complete with cucumber sand-wiches—Sondra berated the poor servant quite viciously over a small dent in the teapot. Her manner would vacillate between colonial-style patronizing and ranting over some small infraction, and all the while she'd attempt to present herself as the perfectly poised diplomatic wife. I would write letters to my mother about the woman's irrational behavior and the effect of it on all of us. Meanwhile, Mother was trying to make the best of her time in Stockholm, while regretting that, to some extent, she'd caused the divorce.

By New Year's, 1966, the parties and social life were in full swing. I got to know Dr. Amiri and his wife Lily very well. Every other evening I'd go out with them at to a gathering of some sort: A dance or a dinner at some fabulous restaurant where we were served the famous Iranian Pearl Grey Caviar from the Caspian Sea! New Year's Eve itself was spent dancing at the American Embassy, and what a party!

The Amiris, Said, and me in a Teheran restaurant.

SKF employees; I'm seated center, with the boss standing behind me.

Then, on January 3, it came: the letter from Pan Am. I had been hired, pending medical exams that would be done by a special Pan Am doctor in Teheran. It would be another few months before they'd call me to the United States for my "stewardess training," as it was called.

Through Dr. Amiri and his wife, I met Said, a very nice young Iranian whom I dated for a while. We both spoke French as well as English, and used both to communicate. Said's family lived nearby and he took me to visit them once. I was blindsided by the fact that his father was a staunch opponent of the Shah. In those days that kind of opposition could result in a visit by the notorious Savak Police. Imprisonment and torture were common. It seems such things have always been the case in the Middle East.

One day, I received a call from a management supervisior from Pan Am. Her name was Lee Trujillo, and she was the intended recipient of that small gift I'd been asked to deliver from Stockholm, so I invited her to the residence to collect it. She was very nice, and clearly impressed by the surroundings. When our conversation turned to Pan Am, I asked her what it was like to fly for the airline. "They do complain," she said of the stewardesses, "but the job is what you make of it." That attitude—which seemed distinctly American—was new to me.

Although my evenings in Teheran were quite full, I had no interest in being idle during the day—I wanted a job. So it was arranged for me to work as a secretary at the Swedish ball bearing company, SKF. The office was in the middle of the city, and the boss was a very affable Swedish man. I was placed in front of a typewriter next to another Swedish girl and an American. When I asked the American girl what she thought of Pan Am stewardesses, she replied, "Wellll…they're okay. Nothing special!" In fact, it was the SKF job that was nothing special—but it gave me one more experience to add to my resume. And then came another opportunity.

In my mind I was still a model, and in Paris, in addition to my job at the fashion house, I had done a lot of pret-a-porter (ready-to-wear) presentations. One day during my Teheran stay, an Iranian lady asked me if I wanted to model her collection of evening dresses, and I accepted her offer immediately. One of the creations I modeled was a red dress that I liked very much. Payment for my services had never been discussed but I took it for granted that she would pay me, and she did—with the red dress! I was aghast, and Sondra wrote her a letter stating that cash payment was expected. She insisted on sending the red dress back to the lady, who was very upset at the gesture. "Oh, but I thought she liked the dress so much," she exclaimed. I have to give Sondra some credit for standing up to the woman.

The day came when I was to meet the Pan Am doctor. He was a low-life who referred to the airline as "my baby." Pan

A date with an Iranian—dinner only!

Am had a lot of hangers-on in those days, who would take advantage. My "exam" was odd and very superficial, and the doctor offered nothing but lip service about the flying job. I finally got rid of him and was given a clean bill of health.

Just for the record, my father was also the Swedish envoy to Afghanistan, so he visited Kabul and many other sites there. My book about him includes a picture of him stretched out serenely on a carpet in a mountainous area, surrounded by Afghani traders in kaftans and turbans. It was a more peaceful time, and Father loved it there. He wrote several books about his various diplomatic posts, including Iran and Afghanistan. I never got to visit Afghanistan, but remained in Teheran until the day I was contacted by Pan Am and told to report promptly for training in Miami.

Sondra had a little Shitzu dog named Madam Wong of Chasmu . . . yes! She was a temperamental little thing, and had a penchant for chewing—and choking on—cotton wool, taking after her neurotic mistress, no doubt. "Madam Wong, Madam Wong, sit still," my father would demand, to no avail.

The dog adored only one person and it was not Sondra. It was a kindly gentleman from the Embassy staff who would visit now and then. She would jump up on him, lick him, and charm him. I think she was drawn to his calm demeanor, which made him quite the opposite of the mistress of the house, with her uncontrolled outbursts.

My brother told me that I missed many of Sondra's episodes when I was out for the evening with the Amiris or Said. She would scream out in anger and wreak havoc on the house. Once, she started fires in a closet and a bathroom. On another occasion, she grabbed a pair of scissors and cut up one of my father's suits. She was jealous of my mother and of Mrs. Pousette. Twice, she tried to commit suicide and was hospitalized. Once, she gave my brother a little "present" of a lock of her hair and asked him to keep it after her death.

Eventually, my father had had enough of her. Although he pitied her, could not tolerate his wife meddling in the affairs of the Swedish Foreign Office. When the sedate Swedes let it be known that Sondra's behavior was not acceptable, my father had to take a stand.

It was all leading to a divorce, and it was very painful for all involved. Sondra had been divorced twice before in South Africa, and her family in England was well aware of how difficult she was. In retrospect, I think that she may have been bipolar. Sadly, it was my little brother who bore the brunt of her temperamental outbursts on a daily basis—especially when my father took a short trip to Sweden and I had already departed for America. Carl Gustaf disliked Sondra so much that he got physically ill from the ordeal. To this day, he mentions it from time to time.

It isn't as if Sondra was trying to be a miserable witch. In fact, she attempted to endear herself to him—calling him "Master" and all that—but her efforts failed miserably. Thankfully, Carl Gustaf had a very nice teacher who rescued him and let her stay with her until his departure for Sweden.

I met someone rather interesting at one of those black-tie events. His name was Darius and right away I thought he looked a little bit out of place. He had a kind of craggy face, like someone who would play a hitman in a spy movie. Well, that turned out not to be far from the case. We started going out and one evening he took me to his office. He said he was in the advertising business, and showed me some kind of board room with an oval table and chairs all around, but he looked a bit unfamiliar with the place. *This is no businessman,* I thought. Anyway, we had a good time together and he followed me all the way to the United States, to the Miami training school, no less. How he could get away from his job and pay for the expensive airline ticket I had no idea, but I didn't think much about it. I was with Pan Am, and nothing else mattered.

A few years later, I was told by someone who knew him that he was an agent for the CIA. I never saw him again, and sometimes wonder what happened to him when the revolution began. After that, Americans, their spies, and Pan Am were no longer welcome in Iran.

On the day the call came from Pan Am that I should report to Miami for training, I hurried over to the American embassy to get my visa. I got there just a few minutes before it would close for the day. My time in Teheran was coming to an end, and an entirely new phase of my life was beginning.

On April 19, 1966—a most memorable day—I arrived in the United States. My diplomatic background was in my past, never to be revisited. I'd enjoyed a privileged lifestyle filled with adventure and exotic lands in what we call today the "third world." At that time, these cultures were admired. My memories of Africa and Teheran—as well as Paris and Berlin—will always be with me. Sweden was another story, set apart from the rest. Perhaps that's because I'm Swedish-born, and it was all a little too close for comfort. Throughout all those years, I was dancing around the edge, never quite belonging, but nonetheless enjoying a special freedom that most people only dream about.

Now, I was entering a new world across the Atlantic, in First Class on a Pan Am flight.

Chapter Thirteen

The World's Most Legendary Airline

1966-1970 SAN FRANCISCO

"Y̶ou have nice legs!" commented the immigration officer with an approving smile. Now I knew I was in America. The ready wit, the complete lack of formality, the quick repartee, the energy, and especially the positive "can-do" attitude were things I was encountering for the first time in my life. These attitudes are quintessentially, uniquely American. This kind of spirit exists nowhere else in the world, period.

April 19, 1966, the day I arrived at JFK Airport, was registered on my Alien Registration Card—my so-called Green Card. It would be several years before I decided to become a U.S. citizen. During the last century, resident aliens were treated like citizens, and many never bothered to complete the paperwork and the very long waiting period it took to change their status. The only drawbacks, of course, were not being able to vote or serve on jury duty.

April 19, 1966, was also my official "date of hire" at Pan American, and it would stay with me throughout my employment as my so-called "seniority date." This date was important, as it came into play when bidding for desirable international routes and qualifying for time off and raises in pay scale. The more senior I became, the more control I had over my life.

I checked into a hotel by the airport, according to my instructions, and the next day I was on my way to the infamous training school in Miami. I wrote in depth about my experiences there in *Glamour and Turbulence*, so I'll just touch on the ordeal here.

Embarking on my new adventure was a bit of a shock to the system and, after the strenuous and very long flight from Teheran, I found myself bedridden with a massive migraine. I thought this would be the end of me, but a nice doctor gave me a powerful injection of some kind of painkiller and I recovered quite nicely. Here I was, in a Miami Airways Motel with four trainees to a room and airplanes roaring above us. Contrary to the supposed glamour of the job, this felt like the all-time opposite. Fortunately, I had been warned that this was just a trial period; the great lifestyle wouldn't come until much later.

First, we were given all the shots—yellow fever, tetanus, cholera, and smallpox. With our arms still sore, we spent the next four weeks being bombarded with safety training: evacuation procedures, ditchings, decompressions, fires on board, and how to use three types of fire extinguishers. We learned about first aid and a wide variety of medical emergencies—including childbirth—and we became familiar with oxygen bottles, life rafts, and other survival equipment. The hardest part of the training was memorizing the locations of all those safety items, since we had to be able to grab them in darkness and/or smoke conditions. Service procedures were taught for just one week, as these particular skills were best learned on board. There were written tests every day, and anyone who didn't pass them was terminated. This was all part of a probation period that would last an agonizing six months. During that time, we wore badges that said "trainee" and were treated like inferiors. Ah, the good old days!

My "check flight" was to London, and it was an absolute disaster! I was airsick nearly the entire time, and had to just sit there on a jump seat. The crew just left me alone and no reports were made about my performance. My classmates got rave reviews. I don't know how I made it to graduation, but I learned to SMILE.

Here we are in our class picture, taken on the steps of the training school building. All thirty of us are decked out in our iconic dove-blue gabardine uniforms, white gloves, sixties pill-box hats, and regulation high-heeled pumps of two-to-three inches. We proudly display silver wings on our lapels; the gold ones would be awarded only after our six-month probation period.

Yes, we'd completed tests and engaged in rigorous safety training maneuvers. We'd jumped into life rafts and slides, and evacuated in smoke—but we also had to look good. Under our impeccable, conservatively fitted uniforms, we had to wear five pieces of underwear: a full bra, full slip, panties, hose, and the infamous girdle. Red or coral lipstick and nail polish finished the look. The only time we were ever permitted to drink Champagne while in uniform was at our graduation reception.

By the time we were done, I had had quite enough of the horrible training, as well as the horrible hotel that served the most tasteless food I had ever eaten. I was quite done with the lizards by the pool and the men of all kinds ogling us during our brief attempts to bask in the sun. Their interest in dating us was confounded by our evening curfews and the tremendous amount of study we had to do before we turned in early in order to be fresh for the next day.

Let me add that we were paid during our training period, and could be promptly fired for minor infractions. We all understood that we could be replaced quite easily by one of thousands of applicants—not just in the U.S. but all over the world. There was no shortage of young, well-educated, and multi-lingual girls wherever Pan Am interviewed, including Europe, Japan, and South America.

The next phase of the Pan Am experience was determining the base location from where we'd fly. As I recall, we could make requests and were then awarded a location based on our language abilities and the needs of Pan Am. The potential bases were New York, San Francisco, Los Angeles, Houston, Miami, Honolulu, and, for a while, Hong Kong and London. I was very, very lucky in that I got the location I wanted: San Francisco. At the time, the city was a very desirable place to live, and the Pacific, Far East, Australia, and New Zealand routes were some of the best flying in the world. I could never have imagined how rewarding my experiences and adventures would be.

Once my six-month probation period was up, I really started to enjoy my life of exotic layovers, seven- to ten-day trips, weeks of time off, shopping, dining, and sunbathing. Pan Am spoiled its crew members and the glamour was real. We stayed in the finest hotels in the world, including Hiltons and Intercontinentals. Our uniforms were laundered, our suitcases carried for us, and special limos picked us up at the airports. Even our birthdays were celebrated and we enjoyed crew Christmas parties and other celebrations of all kinds, often arranged by the hotels, thanks to the fact that Pan Am, was the most legendary and prestigious airline.

There have been hundreds of books written about this iconic airline, full of fascinating details. Once in a while, on a highway, you might spot a bumper sticker reading, "Pan Am: gone but not forgotten." But…as a friend of mine said recently, "In ten years, there will be very few people who know that there was once an airline called Pan Am." Sad but true.

In June of 1966, the Vietnam war was raging and student demonstrations were igniting streets and campuses around the country. Living in San Francisco, maybe the most progressive and liberal of all U.S. cities, was an eye-opening introduction to

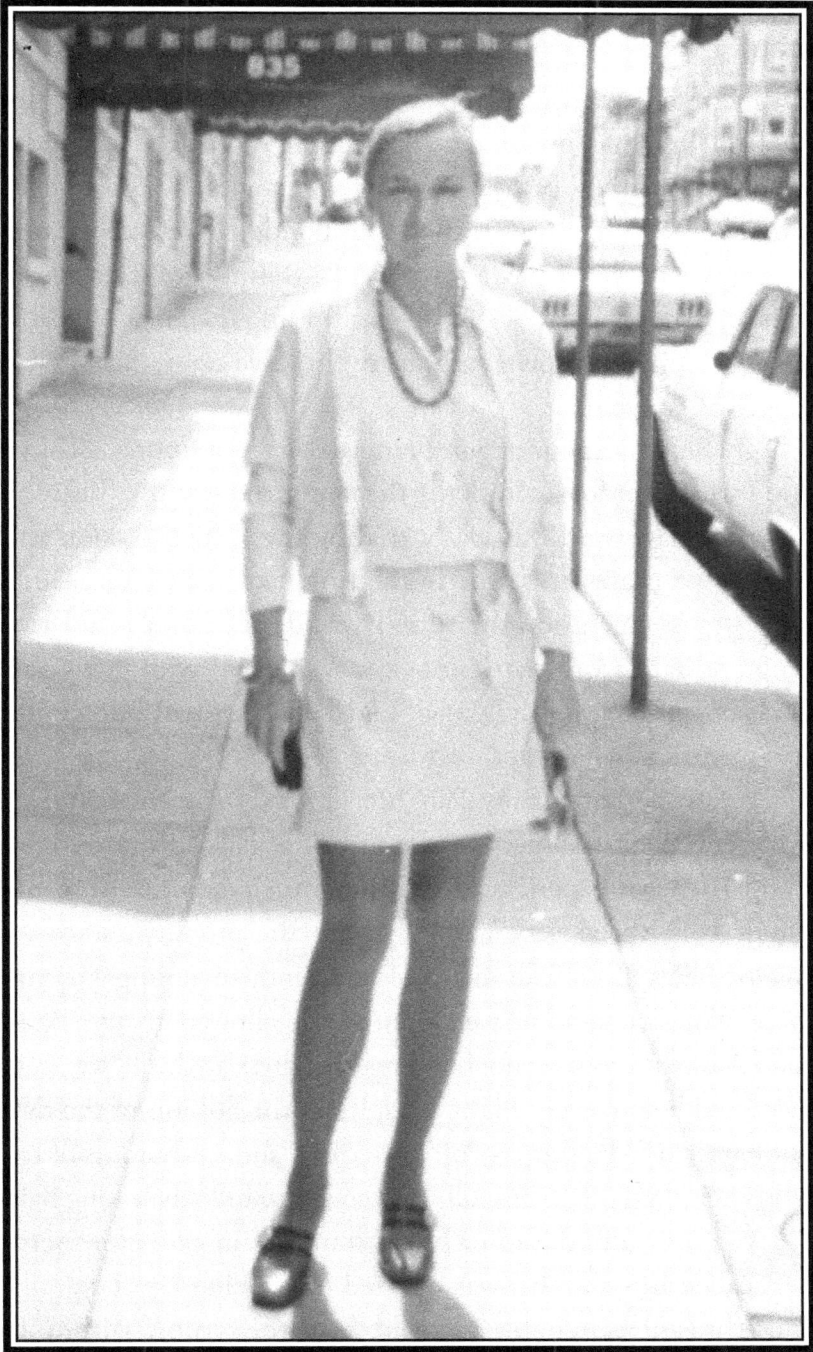

Bush Street, San Francisco, 1966.

life in the U.S. Like my time in Paris, my time in San Francisco was marked by a few address changes between 1966 and 1970. My first home was on Bush Street, in the middle of the city, not far from Union Square. The apartment was adequate, and I lived there with a British girl named Frances, a fellow flight attendant who had been a model in London. We did our best to sightsee in the city when we were at home, going to museums and shops—lots of shops!—and riding the great old cable cars. A ride all over town cost just twenty-five cents and was fun as well as convenient.

My first flight out of San Francisco was ten hours to Tokyo and I will never forget it. Being the new girl, I was the "beanie," or galley slave, and this was a trial by fire. I had to cook and dish up six plates at a time in the tiny back galley, for a total of 120 passengers. By the time I was done—after a full two hours of hard work—my smock was smeared with gravy and I was out of breath. The purser said I'd done okay, but should try to work a little faster next time!

The worst part of my Pan Am days was the air sickness I experienced. But somehow, the grueling galley work—something I'd never experienced—erased my "handicap" from my mind. I had been very worried about the problem, since we weren't allowed to take drugs of any kind, including Dramamine. For that matter, we weren't even allowed to use Band Aids—and there was no bending the dress code as we were inspected before every flight. In spite of the fashion of the day, our hair had to be short—"off-the-collar" short—but lots of the girls, including me, eventually, wore wigs to hide their long hair.

As a new hire, I had to be on stand-by in case crewmembers called in sick. This was referred to as being "in the pool," and it meant being able to make it to the airport within an hour, which was not so easy.

We were expected to arrive promptly for every flight, in regulation uniform, the whole crew with jackets either on or off. On the 707 aircraft, the only equipment we flew in the Pacific, there were six cabin crew members. Our special safety training in San Francisco was conducted by military instructors, and was very good indeed. In a way, the whole Pan Am operation felt like the military. In fact, we flew fly military charters all over the world—the so-called MAC (Military Air Command). In Vietnam, we flew the R & R trips (Rest and Recuperation) for the troops, carrying them to Hong Kong, Taipei, and Australia.

Part of being based in San Francisco was that Honolulu was a kind of second home. It was the first stop and layover for every destination in the Pacific or the Far East. From there, on it was Tokyo or Manila, the Philippines, Guam, Sydney, Auckland, even Wake Island, American Samoa, Djakarta, Singapore, Bangkok, and my two favorite destinations: Tahiti and Hong Kong.

While living in San Francisco, I moved a few times. I left Bush Street after about a year because Frances decided to abandon Pam Am and go back to England. I don't think she cared for the rigors of flying. My next roommate was another colleague, named Ellie, a very accomplished and well-educated girl from the Midwest. She had a teaching degree but wanted to fly for Pan Am.

Ellie and I lived on a typically steep and winding street called Francisco Street. Our second-floor apartment had an amazing view of Alcatraz across the Bay and Fisherman's Wharf just below. This was in the area where they shot the famous car chase scene in *Bullitt*, starring Steve McQueen.

As it was the sixties, I encountered certain individuals of the more radical and anti-establishment kind. Through Ellie, I met a man I'll call Ray, an African American. It seems hard to believe now, but someone at work warned me about the friendship: "What if Pan Am finds out?" That is how conservative and backwards Pan Am could be—even in progressive San Francisco. How times have changed!

Ray was a student at Berkeley, and a true radical revolutionary. He loved talking about eradicating the Establishment. We spent many evenings together in Ellie's and my apartment, talking about the Movement. As another friend of ours once noted, Ray was looking for recruits. He would speak in a slow, deliberate voice about Malcolm X and Eldridge Cleaver, and I would just listen. He was a passionate man, driven by his cause, very serious and genuine, and I had no intention of interrupting him, asking idle questions, or debating the pros and cons of his idealism. I agreed with him for the most part, and the times were changing on so many fronts. Race relations, the Vietnam war, the women's movement were all up for debate. Young people were being guided by their social conscience, and it made us all extremely active.

We had endless conversations into the night, just as young people were doing all over the world. It made me think back to the political discussions I'd had in Paris cafes and Stockholm coffee houses. I was hearing a lot of the same kinds of arguments coming from American students now—mainly in reference to the Vietnam war.

A Pan Am pilot named Charlie dated Ellie for a while, and came around to visit us and enjoy a bit of marijuana along with our Chardonnay and cigarettes. I remember the stuff had names like Acapulco Gold and Panama Red, and was quite potent—it hit me *hard*! One time, we were having escargots with garlic and oil for dinner, all of a sudden, the snails were alive on my plate! I kept saying, "They are alive!" and I started literally climbing the wall, literally. After that, I started dancing.

From then on, every time I had a few puffs of a joint I'd start dancing in our living room, sometimes with a cane, a la Bob Fosse, or in a grass skirt I'd picked up in Tahiti, accompanied by recordings of Tahitian drums. I still loved dancing and had resumed my modern dance lessons at a studio in San Francisco.

I once had mescaline and had a beautiful experience out in the surroundings of the city. I found the effect of that drug very smooth and serene, but once was enough for me. In those days, there was no such thing as drug testing, and at Pan Am we never discussed what we did in our free time. We did, however, talk a lot about the legal drugs we were taking. Those Pacific flights were seven to ten hours long with no rest breaks, so we sometimes resorted to Dexedrine—"uppers"—to stay awake. We had no idea how dangerous and addictive the little pills could be. The frequent time changes and constant jet lag were a constant part of our lives, and, although I tried to sleep for ten or twelve hours straight on layovers and at home, those little green capsules came in very handy.

Then came one of the most earth-shattering experiences I have ever taken part in. One night, at Ray's apartment in Sausalito, he and I did LSD. He had assured me I would be okay and not go crazy or jump out a window—the things I'd heard about. But, just in case, he had a tranquilizer if needed.

The LSD tablet, which looked like pressed oregano, was cut in half and we each took our portion. After about forty-five minutes, the walls and carpet started to sway and shimmer. I had a blue Australian opal ring on my finger, and it became the ocean! Time stood still. I was in another world, a world of colors and shadows, and nothing seemed important anymore. Ray and I sat there, hypnotized, and of course Ray talked about revolution. I could hear what he was saying, and it all sounded very sweet and innocent.

Ray remained cool and calm, always, which is why I

enjoyed his company so much. Of course, beneath that sooth-ing voice were undertones of his struggle. He'd allow himself to enjoy a good meal, but he'd say, "First comes the fight . . . but in the meantime . . . *food*!

In order to keep up with his ideas, I read books by and about Eldridge Cleaver, Malcolm X, and the Chicago Seven. We listened to Aretha Franklin. It was the sixties! I will never forget Ray. He once came to see me in New York in the early seventies, and mentioned something about a shoot-out he had been involved in. To this day, I'm not sure whether he ever did time, but he talked a lot about the FBI, and how there were surveillance cameras hidden around New York. He even told me that the FBI had a modeling shot of me! He claimed he'd become a photographer as some kind of cover. I never saw him again after that visit.

Ellie was a neutral spirit, tending not to side with anyone polit-ically or otherwise, but she certainly was a democrat. Most of us were, including Katarina, a Swedish colleague at Pan Am. Refer-ring to some of the more radical flower children in the Haight Ashbury District, she once said, "It would be fun to live in a tree!" Mainly, though, the hippies lived in communes. I met some of them and I must say, it would have been easy to drink that Kool-Aid. There were just so many drugs.

My LSD trip would never be repeated. As I was slowly com-ing down from it the next morning, a rather frightening thing occurred. If you've experienced LSD, then maybe you felt some-thing similar: a kind of blockage of the brain where time just stops. There I was, back home in my kitchen, and I was unable to put my arm down. It was as if it was frozen in midair. After a few moments, I finally got it down, but I couldn't make myself fry an egg. It was as if I had been stricken with catatonia.

Eventually, I got into bed and slept for nine hours, woke up for a little while, then slept for another eight hours. Finally, I felt like myself again. If you want to experiment with drugs, you'd better know what you are doing—but I must say I found the experience interesting, and I don't regret it.

Flying out of San Francisco was fantastic, but being a flight attendant was never stimulating enough for me on its own. Luckily, I had an inordinate amount of free time, so I could pursue other interests. Many crew members spent their time off traveling, either home to their families or on adventures around the world—exploring the Amazon, climbing mountains in Tibet, that sort of thing. Some had little side businesses buying and selling goods from around the world, never mind customs regulations.

I decided to try modeling again, so I visited a local modeling agency I had heard about called La Vonne Valentine. What a farce that turned out to be! The proprietor was a middle-aged lady who claimed to have important contacts all over San Francisco, and promised me all kinds of modeling jobs.

One day, a few of us models were invited to a party in an upscale part of the city. We were told it would be attended by many prominent people and important photographers. When we arrived, the hostess sized us up and down and made comments like, "Oh, very pretty," as if we were on display. The whole thing was very silly, and the only photographer I saw was an old man on crutches! I got one job through La Vonne Valentine, and that was a pret-a-porter showing by visiting New York designers and sales people. I did enjoy my return to modeling for a few days—until I heard the truth about my lady Valentine: She was an *old hooker*!

My sessions with her ended soon enough, but I did manage to get some pictures taken of me that I still have, in a suit, dress, and bikini. I also got a head shot on glossy paper with a

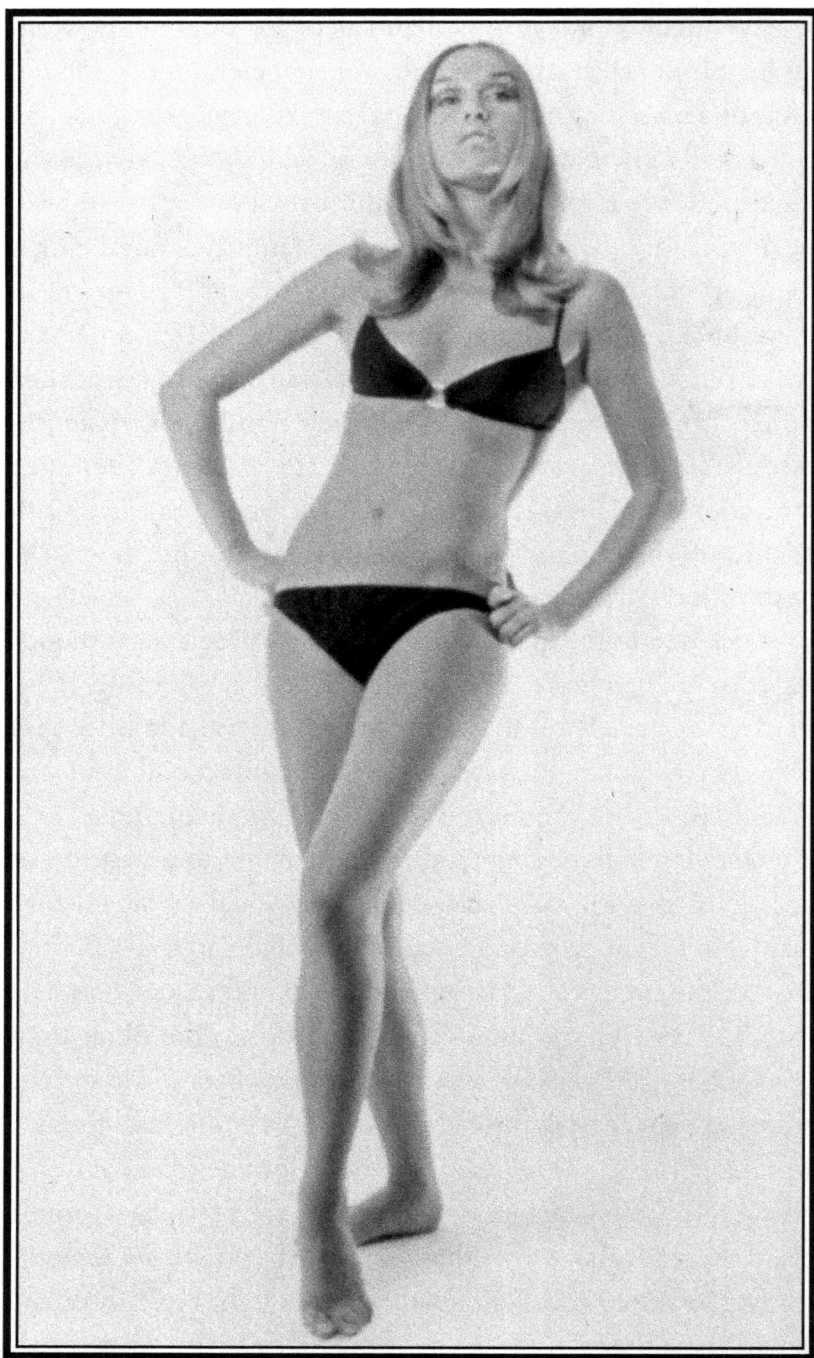

Vintage model shot, à la 1966.

so-so resume on the other side. It is fun to look at those sixties shots now, very posed and stiff.

My San Francisco years were significant to me because they were my first four years in the United States, and my years of flying the Pacific. It truly was the Golden Age of aviation, much more glamorous than today's form of travel, where luggage has to be crammed above your seat and upgrading to First Class is an ordeal. Passengers didn't think about those things then. They didn't have to settle for a choice of peanuts or pretzels, or watch a flight attendant lug a grey garbage bag down the aisle to collect the trash.

It's a shame that the industry and its employees have lost respect, as they are every bit as qualified as we were then. Today, the public seems to be unaware that in-flight crew members are FAA certified and well-trained in safety protocols. Only the best trainees make it to graduation. The sophistication of air travel may be a thing of the past, but the high quality of the personnel is not. I wish these hard-working people were called flight AGENTS, instead, since they represent the company and must adhere to its standards. The title "attendant" does not inspire respect, and I don't think "steward" or "hostess" are much better.

By 1970, I was ready to leave San Francisco and the West Coast, but before heading east, I did have some wonderful and unforgettable times in Tahiti, Hong Kong, and Taipei. I also had family in Los Angeles—my uncle Carl and his wife Lois, who are no longer with us—with whom I had many memorable visits. They have three children, my cousins Anna Lisa, Ingrid, and Bengt. Throughout my San Francisco years, I visited them often, sometimes with my mother and younger brother. My Aunt Lois was a formidable hostess, accom-

A San Francisco cable car.

plished author, former journalist, and eventually, the matri-arch of the family. The parties she arranged were unforgettable—often in celebration of her husband Carl's birthdays—and we were all invited from wherever we happened to be living. I would come in from my layovers in Asia or Africa just to be with this extended family, and I am so grateful for them. They were my sponsors for entry into the United States, and the fun and the joy and the security of having my cousins still with me in the U. S. is wonderful, even though I rarely see them. Bengt is a vagabond of sorts, "dancing around the edge" just as I always have. I love this secondary family as much as I do my other second family in Sweden—my older brother and his sons, Gustaf and Carl Fredrik, and their families. It's a shame we don't see one another more often, but that's the way it has always been with me—dancing around the edge.

A few other San Francisco friends were important to me during this time. There was Cal, a kind and devoted man who enjoyed my company although there was no intimacy or romance between us—just good times. We all have to have a few platonic male friendships, I suppose, to counterbalance the tension and passion of intimate relationships. There are turbulent relationships, hot and painful, and then there are the cooler and calmer ones.

I saw a variety of other men in San Francisco, some significant, others not as much. The details don't need to be shared. There were pilots on layovers and more steady ones that lasted a while. The sixties was a time when young people tended to be very active sexually, some even promiscuously. It was the time of the Pill, before AIDS and concern about sexual harassment, and other harsh realities of today. As a response to the conservative 1950s, we had few inhibitions—call it the sexual revolution—and the traditional roles of mother and wife were not goals but choices. Women could chart their own course. Sweden was far ahead in this, though the U.S. worked hard to keep up.

One boyfriend I had in San Francisco was quite a gentleman. We had some good times in Tiburon, where he lived,

Ghirardelli Square, San Francisco.

Vintage cars, c. 1960.

cooking good dinners inviting friends to come around. I owe my interest in cooking largely to that man. It was not a passionate relationship, however, and it ended soon enough.

My affair with a particular pilot, on the other hand, was a torrid one, if unrewarding in other ways. I do have good memories of this good-looking and worldly man, with whom I parted ways when I moved to New York.

My San Francisco adventure was over, never to be forgotten.

Chapter Fourteen

Drums of Tahiti and Scents of Hong Kong

1966-1970

I have to devote a special chapter to my favorite destinations with Pan Am—Tahiti, Hong Kong, Taipei, and Tokyo—having mentioned them only briefly in *Glamour and Turbulence*. Among all of my layovers in Europe, South America, the Middle East, and even Africa, these four destinations stand out and hold very special memories for me.

This was the "Golden Age of Aviation," and for many years we flew only Boeing 707 aircraft in the Pacific. We were six cabin crew members—three in first class and three in economy—out of which two were pursers, a senior one and a junior one. The cockpit crew consisted of a captain, a first officer, and a navigator. On long trips of seven to ten days, the crew usually stayed together, and we got to know one another quite well. On our two-to-four-day layovers, romances and affairs were common.

There were crew parties all the time, and Christmas and birthday celebrations were often arranged by the first-class hotels where we stayed. Our uniforms were laundered and our bags carried. In those days, we packed large suitcases for ten-day trips.

You could say we were spoiled. When we checked into our hotels, little yellow "per diem" envelopes were waiting at the desk with enough money not only for meals but a certain amount of shopping, too! On one of my first trips to Manila, the purser commented about her crisply starched blouse, fresh from the laundry, "Not such a good job, is it?!" As a new hire, I thought she was being very petty! I'd soon learn that everything had to be perfect, just as our service on board did. For example, the parsley on the passengers' plates had to be placed at the "five o'clock" position exactly. I won't dwell further on the famously exacting Pan Am Service here, but if you are interested, you can read all about it in my Pan Am book.

Our first layover on any Pacific trip was, as I mentioned before, always Honolulu, Hawaii, which became a second home. We stayed at the Royal Hawaiian Hotel, a pink building with palm trees all around it and strobe lights that added drama and romance. And then there was the beach! Stretches of sand and azure blue water where we lay around all day in our bikinis. (This was a time before people worried about sun damage—or the effects of smoking and drinking, for that matter.) In the evening, we got together in some restaurant close by, and I remember the meals were often "surf and turf," wonderful seafood and steaks, along with many glasses of wine. We were often entertained by popular stars such as Don Ho, hula dancers, and a variety of other great Hawaiian music. Around our necks, we wore the decorative garlands called leis.

Our next destination was the most romantic and beautiful place in the Pacific: Tahiti. There were of course other islands where we had frequent layovers, including Guam and American Samoa, but Tahiti was special.

After checking into the hotel in Papeetee, we would board a small ferry boat to go to the famous island of Moorea, where three American guys named Muck, Kelly, and Jay had a hotel by the name of Bali Hai. They'd bought the land from the French Government and had built the exotic resort, which consisted of many Tahitian huts that functioned as hotel rooms. Dining was done in an open area, where wonderful fish dishes and coconut and pineapple sides were served. Best of all, next to a little fishpond was a dance floor surrounded by rattan chairs. All evening long, Tahitian drummers played the most seductive and sensual music. Clad in our "pareos"— short pieces of flowery cotton fabric wrapped around our hips, usually matching our bikini tops—and with leis over our shoulders and hibiscus flowers behind our ears, we would dance to the drums all night long! The men wore shorts, flowery shirts, and leis as well.

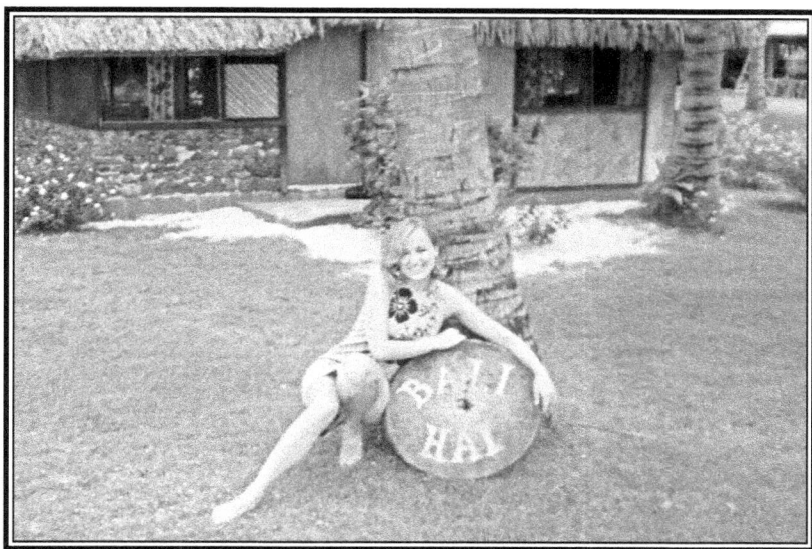

Relaxing in Bali Hai

The dance we did was the Tahitian hula, performed much more quickly than the Hawaiian version, moving side to side with bent knees. There was a special night club of sorts called the One Chicken Inn, where Marlon Brando and his *Mutiny on the Bounty* film entourage used to hang out. There was a story about how the place got its name by serving hundreds of people with ONE chicken—and I'll leave it at that. All I know is that on that clay floor, I danced to the drums and drank Rusty Nails until morning. There were always a number of locals collapsed over the tables from an excess of drink. As for us crew members, we were young and could hold copious amounts of liquor! Even so, stories circulated about both pilots and stewardesses who'd overdone it on layovers, because, in those days there was no drug or alcohol testing. At least one book by a pilot reveals that flight accidents did happen—but this was all a very long time ago.

My next favorite layovers were Hong Kong and Taipei. These were the rest-and-recuperation destinations for our troops in Vietnam. Flying the R&Rs was part of being employed by Pan Am. We were issued the Geneva Card which, in case of capture, was meant to protect us against abuse. According to the Geneva Convention, those in possession of the card had only to state their names and employment numbers, and would automatically be awarded "officer status."

We flew into Saigon, Danang, and Kam Rhan Bay, where we picked up the GIs—General Infantry—and took them to Hong Kong and Taipei, or down to Darwin, Australia.

Danang, 1967.

Although the R&R flights were short, the layovers were long enough to enjoy. We would fly two legs back and forth and then enjoy two full days in one of the destination cities.

Hong Kong was magic, beginning with the pungent smell of the harbor that hit us as we disembarked from the aircraft. The landing was always difficult for the pilots, who had to maneuver around hills in order to land on a steep, short strip that ran between high buildings. As always, we stayed at the best hotels—including the Mandarin, where we enjoyed a traditional breakfast of thin orange crepes—the best in the world!

Hong Kong was a mecca of beautiful shops filled with jade and Australian opals. There were tailors who'd measure us for custom outfits and even boots. Once, a good friend of mine by the name of Gunilla was being fitted for a special suit. "Oh, Mr. Wong," she commented, "the side here is not straight! Mr. Wong, look…" Of course Mr. Wong was ever so obliging and dignified. It was all great fun. We'd spend our days running in and out of tempting little shops, looking at jewelry and Chinese robes and slippers and eyeglass holders and imaginative ornaments of all kinds. On one such trip, I acquired a beautiful scarlet robe that I kept for years, which a friend with a sense of humor referred to as my "madam robe." Actually, many of the things that could be had in Hong Kong looked like they belonged in opium dens or quaint bordellos!

On one of my Hong Kong layovers, I was introduced to a very special person named Gerald Godfrey, and his Chinese friend. Gerald was one of the most interesting characters I had ever met on all my travels. I spent many layovers in that spectacular city with Gerald and his friend, along with fellow crew members. Never had I tasted Peking duck as good as what we had. In fact, all of the Chinese food I enjoyed there was the best I will ever have in my life.

Gerald lived in the New Territories, in a villa on a hill that he called "The Monastery," though I have no idea why. We were invited up there a few times and it was like stepping into a world of mystery and magic. Everywhere you looked were porcelain cats, purple brocade curtains, Chinese scrolls and screens, black satin, scarlet satin, tassled pillows of more brocade, high-poster beds with gilded posts, Chinese carpets all colors, lacquer, and other beautifully crafted things. Gerald had five dogs, one of which he'd named the Little Whore. She was a fluffy and scruffy little beauty who shared his attention with three other mutts of various types. They ran all over the overgrown garden. The whole experience was like an irresistible adventure. And then came the food! Gerald would set before us a feast of Chinese delicacies that we enjoyed while gazing out at our colorful surroundings and breathing in the fresh mountain air. It was unforgettable.

Taipei was another mysterious city. I actually do not have too many memories of the place. I do remember the million bicycles in the streets, and the rickety-dickety taxis we'd ride all over town. There was wonderful food, of course, and shopping, and I especially remember a kind of "dragon show," with mysterious dancers moving to shrill music, performing with masks and elongated fingernails.

We stayed in a Hilton hotel there. One star-spangled night, we were invited up to the top of a hill for a Mongolian Barbecue. We had a magnificent view of the Imperial Palace set against the midnight-blue sky, and were served one of the tastiest meals I've ever had. It consisted of four kinds of meat—venison, lamb, beef, and pork—cut up in little pieces and placed in a bun and garnished with fifteen kinds of sauces, including sesame and ginger and all the other flavors of the

Far East. Dining under that starry sky in that fresh midnight air was something I will never forget.

My fourth favorite destination was Tokyo, where I spent many layovers between 1966 and 1970. After I transferred to New York in 1970, I continued to fly there until 1984, for a total of eighteen years.

The flights from San Francisco to Tokyo always stopped in Honolulu for twenty-four-hour layovers. Out of New York, we laid over in either Fairbanks or Anchorage, then continued on to Tokyo. Either way, we flew only about seventy hours a month, which amounted to about two weeks gone. The rest of the time, we were off! How can you beat that?

A friend and Pan Am colleague named Eva was offered a career with a top modeling agency in the 1970s. She could make a lot of money, she was told, but she'd have to quit Pan Am. Guess what? She wasn't interested. That was the power of our company. We loved our lifestyle, and we "tough-loved"

Eva Jorgensen, 1970s; Eva and me in the galley, 1990.

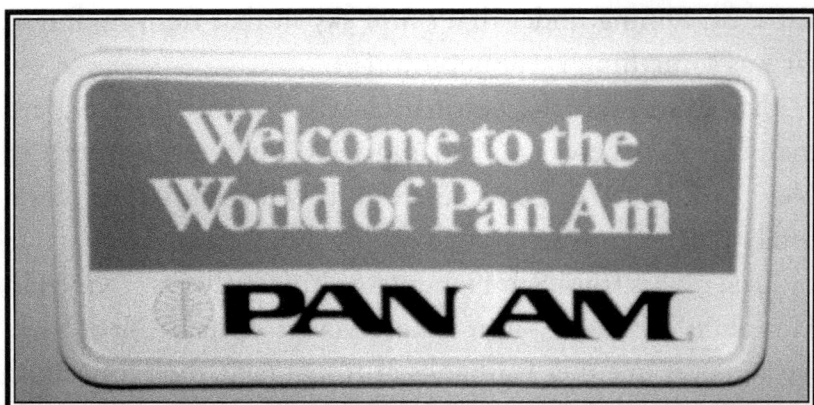

Pan Am sign on an airplane door.

Pan Am. In spite of the troubles the company had in the early seventies, nobody ever quit. There was a general hope that the airline was too big to fail—and, amazingly, it did continue to fly for another twenty years, until December 1991.

In Tokyo, which I have written about more extensively in my previous book, we availed ourselves of the fabulous shopping at the Oriental Bazaar, loading up on lampshades, porcelain pots, screens, scrolls, jewelry, kimonos—new as well as antique—lacquerware, and the famous "Tokyo Bags" made of nylon that were so strong they lasted for years. In the department stores, we shopped for humidifiers, answering machines, and cameras. One pilot even purchased a motorcycle and put it in the belly of the aircraft. I once purchased a strand of baroque Tokyo pearls for ninety dollars and sold it a few years later in New York for nine hundred.

We feasted on Shabu Shabu, Sushi, and Korean barbeque and sipped sake in the little eating spots on narrow side streets. I had my hair expertly cut and styled at the Keio Plaza Hotel, and indulged in heavenly shiatsu massages—a godsend after a long flight.

After sleeping for twelve hours, I would have a breakfast in my room of coffee, dainty little cinnamon buns, and sliced bananas with cream. A few hours later, I would join the crew in the main dining area for a larger breakfast—really, my lunch—and then we'd all head out on shopping sprees.

At the entrances of the magnificent department stores we were greeted by bowing ladies in uniform. The apples and other fruits for sale were wrapped in silk paper and tied with bows. Have you ever heard of that? Was there ever a city like that? This was Tokyo then. After Pan Am, I never revisited this fascinating metropolis, but my memories remain, along with my admiration for the Japanese people: their gentleness, kindness, intelligence, integrity, and industriousness. Some war veterans of World War II might see it differently, but that is another story and I respect their point of view.

In Tokyo on a layover, a certain serenity would come over me. When Pan Am discontinued those flights from New York, I found myself at a total loss as to where I would fly. That was in 1984, the year my mother died suddenly at age sixty-nine. I felt that the world had ended a little. The joy was gone. It would take me a full two years to recover.

On a very happy note, however, years before that time, something quite wonderful happened. It was 1969, and my father had been appointed Swedish Ambassador to Dublin, Ireland. He was divorced from Sondra, who eventually moved back to London, having received a good settlement from my father. I was flying for Pan Am, and was able to visit both Sweden and Ireland from time to time. My younger brother, now thirteen, was going to school in Dublin and was with my parents all the time. My mother had joined my father in Ireland, and one day, as my brother recounts, he came home from school to find them both sitting at the kitchen table, drinking some wine and having a little lobster dinner. He asked what the occasion was, and my father answered quietly, with a hint of humor, "We got married today—Mother and I!"

Carl Gustaf cried! The Irish priest there had thought it peculiar that my mother and father wanted to get married. In his view, they were already married, and had been since their first ceremony in 1939 in Copenhagen.

All was well.

Chapter Fifteen

"The Great Big Witch on the Hudson"

1970-90 NEW YORK

In March of 1970, I arrived in the most exciting city in the world. If you are wondering, my chapter title refers to a depiction of New York from the 1900s. It caught my attention when I saw it on a public television show. New York in that era had not been a very democratic place, and someone had done a political drawing showing it as a great big witch looking mean and frightening. In one hand she held the privileged and fortunate, caressing them lovingly with the other. On her body, the middle class rested comfortably while the lower-middle class clutched her sides and legs, trying to climb higher. Finally, by her feet crouched "*les miserables*," the disadvantaged, sick, and hungry, all struggling to survive. Cruelly, she is shown lifting up one foot to step on them and crush them to death!

This was what life was like for many in the early part of the Industrial Revolution, before the Labor Movement and Social Security. Waves of immigrants flooded in through Ellis Island, only to be exploited in sweatshops and factories. The PBS program told the story of the Triangle Shirtwaist Factory fire, a tragic event in which scores of women garment workers, trapped in a burning building with locked exits and no fire escapes, were forced to throw themselves out of windows to their death. Without the protection of unions, these workers—and thousands of others in a variety of industries—worked in unsafe conditions for egregiously low pay. Anyone who tells me that he or she doesn't believe in labor unions had better think again! I believe strongly that unions have bettered the lives of the middle class and improved conditions for all workers over the years. I can tell you firsthand that union workers fare much better in all respects, as I myself have belonged to two of them. At Pan Am, I was a proud member of the flight attendants union, known as the IUFA, and as an actor I was a member of the Screen Actors Guild—and did very well indeed. Unions are necessary!

My first apartment in New York was on the second floor of a small walkup on Third Avenue and Sixty-fifth Street. Being so

New York City phone booth, c. 1970.

close over the street it was noisy and dirty, and ten to twenty roaches inhabited the scruffy little kitchen at any given time. I took it over from a Pan Am colleague who was moving to the West Coast just as I was coming from there. So, here I was in the most exciting place in the world, but my standard of living was now considerably lower than it had been in San Francisco. If you wanted to live in New York at that time, you had to suffer its inconveniences: crime-ridden streets, garbage, noise, crowds, muggings, rudeness . . . perhaps that all sounds terrible, but it was all wonderful! You see, *behind* the dirty facades there was *quality*. The shops, the restaurants, Broadway, the art galleries, Wall Street, Central Park, the Avenues, and above all, the opportunity to succeed in one's chosen field, whether it was the arts, advertising, publishing, or any number of other things.

I appreciated all that New York had to offer, and although I was still flying for Pan Am as a Purser, I was quick to embark on other ventures as well. With fervor, I returned to my jazz dancing lessons. I studied cooking at the YWCA and even took philosophy courses at Hunter College. I also made the rounds of various modeling agencies, with more or less success.

So, I was settling down in my little abode, filling the two small rooms with furniture from the Salvation Army. The décor was "slum baroque," as one friend put it. The most important piece—the bed—was decent enough, and I added odds and ends purchased at the fabulous Macy's. My rent was in the realm of $200 a month, and my landlady...well, she was something else! She called herself "Mrs. Fred" and was a rather theatrical Hungarian lady with brassy blond hair and a comical accent. Her sentences always ending in, "You understand?"

What I had to understand was a truckload of papers she handed me to sign regarding the apartment key, insurance, all kinds of business matters. When I visited her in her rather quaint little studio on Park Avenue to finalize the arrangement, she opened the door clad in a black lacy negligee. "You understand?" What a character she was!

The lease on my modest little hovel was for one year, and I had lived there for just a week when Mr. X walked into my life. Never in my wildest dreams could I have ever imagined what the future would have in store for me when he walked through the door. Who was this character? He had known the previous tenant for a short time, and suddenly decided to come visit.

I had never met anyone like him in my life—he was the quintessential New Yorker. He spoke fast but used few words, and had this way of keeping very still and gazing at me, which made me a tad uncomfortable at first. Well...one thing led to another. By the end of our first day together, he was giving me all sorts of advice about the apartment, as well as a lot of general advice about New York. He was quite aggressive and domineering, and I decided I really did not want anything to do with him. He was too overwhelming. Then came that phone call. "When are you and I going to get together, babe?" That made me laugh. *What was this?* Whatever it was, our relationship has lasted *fifty years*!

Mrs. Fred was stingy with the heat. That first winter in New York I froze—until I resorted to turning on the oven and opening the door for warmth. Needless to say, this was a dangerous practice that could have led to a fire. Ultimately, Mr. X rescued me, declaring that I could move into one of the apartments he owned—along with a roommate, if I so desired—for about $400 a month. My time at Mrs. Fred's, surrounded by my "slum baroque" furniture, street noise, and roaches, came to an end after six months. Then as now, Manhattan was one of the most difficult cities in the world in which to find a decent and affordable place to live—so I was grateful to Mr. X.

Apartment Number Two (as I call it) was wonderful, with three big rooms, a huge kitchen with a window, a hallway, and two small bathrooms. It was in an old building with no doorman, but it was very sturdy and well kept, and located right in the middle of the city. I ended up living there for eight years in the seventies, along with a succession of roommates. First, there was Anna, a Pan Am colleague who looked like Bo Derek. After a year, she moved back to Norway, not unlike many Europeans who come to the U.S. but never quite adapt to the culture and end up go back where they came from.

Then there was Maria, another colleague, a temperamental Italian with lively brown eyes. She used the word *stronzi* all the time, an insult I'd prefer not to translate here. Although she swore she would never leave Pan Am, she ended up going off to Australia with an Italian man she'd met.

Next came Annie, a good old friend who flew for TWA. She eventually married a New Yorker and moved to the West Side. Now she lives in Jupiter, Florida, divorced but satisfied. After a thirty-year gap, we have re-established our friendship.

Erica lived with me for a while, quit Pan Am, regretted it, and managed to get rehired. Then she quit again, married, and moved to Boston.

Last but not least came Sally, who made her entrance into Manhattan from Livingston, New Jersey, where she grew up amongst four brothers and parents and went to school. I met her at the office of a showbiz manager I'll call the Buddha, whom I wrote about in my book *The Other Side of Stardom*. This office of sorts was on East 57th Street, and Buddha held court there every day for a variety of would-be actresses and some rather shady producers (or so they called themselves). The man had a great big heart and was my trusted confidant as well as manager. He introduced me to quite a few casting directors, photographers, and agents, and I owe him for that. He arranged for me to get a small part in a low-budget film, as a Swedish model, and that was my entrée into the coveted Screen Actors Guild in 1971. I had no idea at the time that I would be securing a small SAG pension with my twelve credits over the years (ten was the required minimum), but even more rewarding was the excellent medical insurance that I was grandfathered into at age sixty-five, along with Medicare. And what did I get from the airlines? A tiny pension, a so-so 401(k), and no medical coverage whatsoever—after *forty* years in the business!

Back to Sally. She was a very pretty girl (still is), well spoken, with a gift of the gab, gentle manners, and a well-developed sense of humor. She is of Irish/German descent, and was a far cry from Buddha's usual protegées, other than a few Ford models and accomplished TV and film actresses. Some of them did quite well. Anyway, with his help, Sally was admitted into the Screen Actors' Guild also, and got jobs in films, TV shows, soap operas, as well as print jobs and fit-modeling work.

One day at Buddha's place, Mr. X—who used to come and visit there—asked Sally if she was interested in being my roommate. She jumped at the chance gratefully, moved right in, and many funny stories followed.

At Pan Am I was now a purser—a leader of sorts. There was a senior purser and a junior purser, and then, with the arrival of the Boeing 747 in 1970, the cabin crew increased in number to as many as twelve. With 400 to 500 passengers in three classes of service, the duties could be overwhelming—and the pursers were in charge of it all.

I was flying all over the world now. Europe was my least favorite continent, except for the layovers in Rome, Paris, and Lisbon. Later on, I did enjoy my visits to the cities of Eastern

OTHER PURSER' COMMENTS
SERVICE OUTLINE BRIEFING
EMERGENCY REVIEW (5MIN.)
CAPTAIN'S BRIEFING
GALLEY ATTENDANTS TO A/C
ONE HOUR PRIOR DEPARTURE
ENTIRE CREW TO A/C 55MIN.
PRIOR DEPARTURE

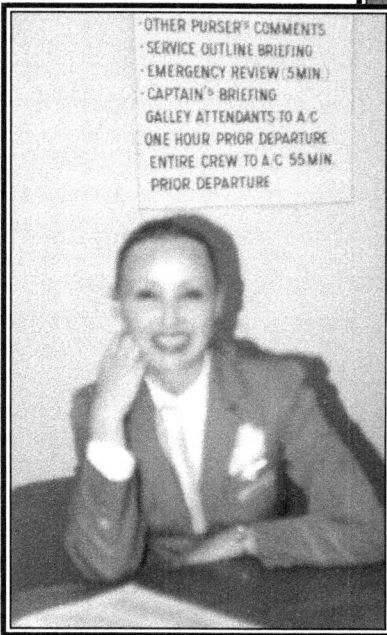

Me as purser in a pre-flight crew briefing; Pan Am uniform, c. 1970.

Europe, such as Budapest and Warsaw. I like Slavic people much more than the Germanic ones, if I may say so. The Gallic, Latin, Celtic, and Anglo-Saxon people have always seemed quite distinctly different to me, although I realize I am running the risk of generalization.

Other destinations in which I enjoyed marvelous layovers were Caracas, Venezuela; Rio de Janeiro and Sao Paulo in Brazil; and Buenos Aires in Argentina. I also flew to the Caribbean, Barbados, Antigua, Tobago, St. Thomas, St. Croix, the

Bahamas, Haiti, the Dominican Republic, and Puerto Rico. The beaches of Antigua . . . what a dream! On a layover once, I got a print job for the hotel, as a tourist in a bikini.

We also flew to Africa—Morocco, Casablanca, Nairobi—but the best was Robertsfield, Liberia, where we swam naked at Caesar's Beach and had the wildest crew parties. It was an infamous layover destination at the time, and rumors of goings-on were numerous. I only flew there twice—not enough to disturb my wonderful memories of Africa's other side—the East coast.

We flew to Beirut, Istanbul, Teheran (again, many memories), Baghdad, and then on to India, New Delhi, and Calcutta. Pan Am offered its famous "Round the World" flights as well as charters. I'll never forget, upon arrival in Venice once, stepping down into a gondola right out of the airplane, suitcases in tow, and heading for our historic hotel. The view as we traveled was like a mirage, something out of a fairytale.

The charter flights could turn into eighteen-hour duty days, and on the 707 aircraft, we had no rest breaks or crew seats, just the uncomfortable jumpseats. In spite of the discomfort, we fell asleep on those!

We flew MAC (Military Air Command) charters all over the world, in and out of any number of war zones. Pan Am was in Tehran during the hostage crisis in the mid-seventies, and rescued the final evacuees of Vietnam. That real-life adventure was turned into a made-for-television movie called *Last Flight Out* in 1990.

In spite of the fact that Pan Am showed signs of failing as a company—and probably would have folded sooner were it not for its famous name—the flying remained great throughout the seventies. At one point, Pan Am seemed to have an unlikely savior when it was rumored that the Shah of Iran might be interested in acquiring it. Needless to say, that didn't happen.

I had one harrowing flight experience I will never forget—on a charter flight from Shannon, Ireland, bound for Philadelphia. As we approached our destination, I was on the back jumpseat along with another crewmember. Suddenly, we were engulfed in a freak storm, and experienced the worst turbulence I ever encountered in forty years of flying. The pilots tried to land six times over the course of two hours, and I honestly believed we wouldn't make it. What does one do in a situation like that? Hold on for dear life and pray it will end well.

Ultimately, we diverted to Washington, and letters and reports were filed about this nightmare. Something had gone wrong. We should have been diverted from the area, as other aircraft were, but we, as well as an Allegheny Airlines flight, were not!

Eventually, I began flying to Tokyo again, out of New York, first on 707s with stops in Anchorage or Fairbanks, and then on the new 747 SPs (Special Performance aircraft that could reach 45,000 feet). Those flights ran twelve-to-fourteen hours non-stop and landed at Narita Airport, followed by a two-day layover. I flew those for fourteen years out of New York, for a total of eighteen years flying to my favorite destination.

I also flew 747 SPs to Saudi Arabia, where, during my layovers, we had to wear loose, modest clothing that covered everything but the face. Full bathing suits were allowed at the hotel pool, during restricted hours for women and children. Likewise, the dining rooms had separate hours for women and men. The Pan Am SPs were taken out of service in 1983.

During my time off—a few weeks per month plus vacations—I enjoyed the wonders of New York and pursued my other budding career: show business. This was always a sideline

—a lark—because I had no intention of quitting my rewarding Pan Am job.

Buddha sent me out on a flurry of activities, including photographer test shots for my modeling book. These included both head and figure shots, in everything from a bikini to an upscale formal dress to a business suit. These would then be presented to the various casting agencies and directors. Armed with my growing book and a bunch of addresses on little slips of paper, I'd make the rounds, trying out for everything from features shooting locally to TV shows, so-called "industrials," commercials, even voiceovers. And of course I continued to pursue print work. Although I have shared many stories from this period in *The Other Side of Stardom*, I cannot write about the seventies in New York without mentioning this aspect of my life, which took up as much of my time as the Pan Am job did. In any given month, throughout the seventies and eighties and even into the nineties, I did at least four or five shoots.

Buddha.

AIMÉE BRATT
LT1-6470

*1970s vintage model shot"; my
headshot for films, complete
with "old-style" contact phone
number, c. 1976.*

Casting directors called steadily, and I had to maneuver this work around my flight schedule —very stressful!

When I'd first arrived in New York, I'd been advised to take acting lessons, something considered to be important for one's resume. Not that acting classes would lead directly to jobs, but they were considered a necessary sign of seriousness and respect for the industry.

I was directed to a certain Brett Warren, an acting teacher who had been blacklisted during the McCarthy era. He held classes at the Ansonia Hotel in the city, under the title, "Actors' Mobile Theatre." I enrolled, and we did plays using the "Method" of Stanislavski. I loved the whole atmosphere.

My first SAG film was called *The Second Coming*. It was a low-budget venture directed by Bob Madero, a very nice and talented man whom I think eventually moved to the West Coast. In my blue silk blouse, hot pants, and platform high-heels, wearing my hair long and blond à la seventies, I was stabbed in the back with a toy knife in a take-off scene of the Manson murders. I was a newcomer, so all that waiting around between shots was a sort of awakening about the business of making movies. I would go on to do some 300 acting jobs, most of them in the background but some with upgrades to lines or silent bits.

The most exciting film I was involved in was *Raging Bull*, in which I played a cigarette girl in the Copa scene. That was followed by *In the Still of the Night*, where I was an auction assistant in a scene with Meryl Streep. I played a receptionist in *Secret of My Success*, a businesswoman in *Baby Boom*, a dream person in *All that Jazz*, a bridesmaid in *Arthur*, a grieving widow in *Devil's Advocate*, and a child-abusing mother in *Presumed Innocent*. In television, I appeared in many episodes of *Law and Order* and *The Equalizer*, the pilot for *Tattingers*, and many others shows.

I also worked on many commercials in rapid succession, thanks to a casting director named Barbara Claman. But, just as quickly as these began, they came to stop. I learned that directors tend to like new faces, so they might use an actor for a period of time and then move on.

I experienced the same phenomenon when posing for book covers. I worked a lot for about a year, and then was considered "old news"—or maybe simply too old. I enjoyed those bookings because the romance covers involved quite a bit of acting with a partner. The photos were then rendered as illustrations.

I do want to talk about one commercial in particular that I

made in the late seventies, when Sally was my roommate. It was for a store on Long Island called Fur Galleria. Today, I am against the use of fur, but we didn't think much about it back then.

On the appointed day, four of us, including Sally and me, were made up to look like cats. Sally was blue-colored, I was green, another model was violet, and the fourth was yellow. The scene was shot on a Lufthansa jet, which was parked on the tarmac at JFK Airport. We were filmed coming out of the airplane in our fur coats, wind blowing.

As we did take after take, the Lufthansa crew let it be known that the allotted time would not be extended; it was time for us to leave—no excuses! The director was not used to being ordered around, but the airline had permitted the shoot as a favor, and he knew that he was lucky to be there at all. I guess he managed to get what he needed, because the commercial aired.

Sally and I would run around the city on "go sees" for photographers and commercial auditions. Some of the potential roles seemed very silly, such as, "Tilly, the manicurist with a German accent." There must have been 100 actresses reading for that one—anyone who could pull off a German accent, regardless of physical type. Since we only got paid if we landed the job,

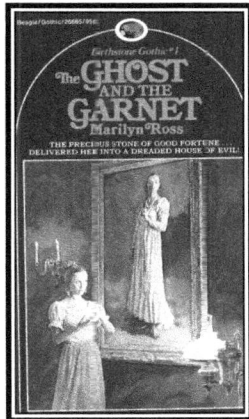

Book covers I modeled for.

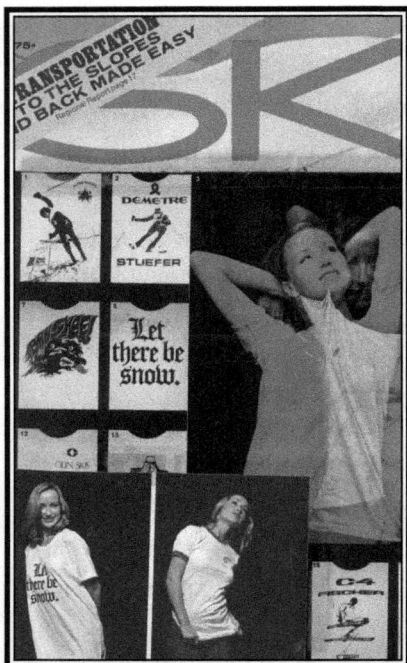

these endless auditions felt like a big waste of time.

I did just a few lingerie modeling jobs. Sally and I went up for the same one once, and I got the booking. It was for a very pointy bra, and the situation became a running joke between us over the years.

The Sally jokes will not be forgotten. Sylvia Fay, a well-known casting director who is

Typical print work.

YOU MUST SEE A DEFINITE SLIMMING OF YOUR WAIST, THIGHS, CALVES, ANKLES, OR YOUR MONEY BACK!
You must see inches of fat literally disappear under the compressive action of Auto-Massage Slimmers. You must be able to measure A DISCERNIBLE DIFFERENCE IN INCHES from tummy, legs, hips, thighs, and ankles...not in days, or even after the first treatment, but from the moment you put them on, or your money back!

Look like the sheerest panty hose.
Wear them day and night!...

see inches disappear from waist, thighs, calves, ankles AT ONCE!

Enthusiastic Acclaim from Doctors and the Overweight Alike!

"I shall be happy to recommend (your method) to my patients."
Dr. J.H., Paris, France

"There is noticeable (impact) in overweight persons who benefit from the *immediate* slimming and shaping effects."
Dr. T.S., Aachen, W. Germany

"Let me confess...I never believed it was possible to see the vast difference you claimed...but it's true! The very first time I put (them) on I looked so slim I had to take them off and put them on again, it was so astonishin'!"
Mrs. V.V., Paris, France

"Thank you! Thank you! Diets and exercise have been a part of my life since I was 18 and I hate them...but with your Slimmers I look better than I ever have before."
Mrs. T.M., Weisbaden, W. Germany

"We just broke the generation gap! My daughter is more than just plump, but she tried them at my suggestion, and now she thinks I'm the world's wisest mother."
Mrs. S.G., Brussels, Belgium

"Miraculous...and they feel so good...you're right, it's just like a comforting massage...and where did all the inches go?"
Miss R.D., Zurich, Switzerland

ERCISES!
The moment you put on your Auto-Massage Slimmers you see results...NO WAITING! They're actually a body-shaping and molding device that gently compress your stomach, hips, thighs, even ankles...look like sheerest panty hose. Simultaneously Auto-Massage action works to increase blood circulation, starts you slimming right away!

Auto-Massage Slimmers trim you instantly, with no effort at all required on your part. As long as you wear them they will continue to fight fat, help keep you slim, five important ways:

AIMEE BRATT
SAG AFTRA

Height: 5'7"
Weight: 127 lbs.
Eyes: Green
Hair: Off Blonde
Dress Size: 8-10
Shoe: 8

FEATURE FILMS - PRINCIPALS

POLLOCK	Pollock Films Inc.
DEVILS ADVOCATE	LowTide Productions
FLY BY NIGHT	FFS Prods.
SCENES FROM A MALL	Fly By Night Productions
PRESUMED INNOCENT	Disney
SEE NO EVIL, HEAR NO EVIL	Warner Bros.
BABY BOOM	Evil Eye Prods.
ME & HIM	United Artists
THE SECRET OF MY SUCCESS	Constantin Films
STILL OF THE NIGHT	Universal
ARTHUR	CBS Theatrical Films
RAGING BULL	United Artists
ALL THAT JAZZ	United Artists
BELL JAR	Columbia
THE SENTINEL	Avco-Embassy
THE FAN	Universal
THE WORLD ACCORDING TO GARP	M.G.M.
ANNIE HALL	Columbia
I COULD NEVER	United Artists
THE SECOND COMING	Ensemble Films
INSIGNIFICANCE	Dobbs Ferry Films
	Zenith Films

FEATURES FOR T.V.

SEVENTH AVENUE	NBC
THE DAIN CURSE	CBS
YOU CAN'T GO HOME AGAIN	CBS
IZZY & MOE	CBS

TELEVISION

LAW & ORDER	NBC
TATTINGER'S	NBC
THE EQUALIZER	CBS
THE HAMPTONS	ABC

T.V. COMMERCIALS

FEDERAL EXPRESS	BBD&O
SONY TV	Hanft Slater Martin
REVLON TEST	Leo Burnett Adv.
KORVETTES	Lois Holland Calloway
SCHLITZ BEER	J.W. Thompson
CASUAL CORNER CLOTHING	Lieber Katz-Adv.
MARINE MIDLAND BANK	Benton & Bowles
DINERS CLUB	Wonderman, Ricotta & Mine
DUPONT	BBD&O
OOMPHIE'S SHOES	Benton & Bowles
COTY PERFUME	Kurtz & Tarlow
JOHNSON & JOHNSON	Compton Adv.
TUFFTIPS NAIL ENAMEL	Joel Holt Prods.
FUR GALLERIA	Jerry Whiteman Prods.
ARROW SHIRTS	Scott Connell Prods.
FASHION CAPERS	Scott Connell Prods.
HANNOVER HOUSE BODYTRIMMER	Beacon Adv.

INDUSTRIALS

AMERICAN EXPRESS	Realty Prods.
PROMOTION FILM FOR CBS - novel "Scruples" (LEAD)	Sotos Prods.
BANKERS TRUST	

VOICE OVERS

BLACK SUNDAY FOR T.V.	Cinecontact

LANGUAGES

SWEDISH (Native) FRENCH (Fluent) GERMAN (Fluent), RUSSIAN (Good Pronunciation)

TRAINING

Brett Warren, Actors Mobile Theatre

An actor's resume.

no longer with us, would frequently call both of us in for feature background work. She was a grand lady, and I appreciated the many jobs she got me throughout the seventies and eighties. It was really Fay who was responsible for securing my SAG pension and excellent Medical Insurance.

Fay was known for her caustic remarks, She once told Sally

to come dressed in an upscale outfit for a scene. "Borrow Aimee's shoes," she told her. "Stewardesses always wear high heels." Another time, she said to her, "Oh, you're the pain in the ass who doesn't like to work in smoke." Right—Sally did not!

During the filming of a scene in *Moonstruck* that took place outside the Metropolitan Opera, she called out, "No rubbers!!" She was referring to the men's shoe protectors, of course; it was a rainy shoot.

A background job with Sally that was not a joke took place in the Hamptons. The film was called *Dying for Love*, but we were dying of cold! Sally and I were positioned on a grassy lawn with two gentlemen. It was supposed to be a summer scene so we had on light summer dresses, but the temperature was in the forties so we bundled up between takes. When they were ready to shoot, the assistant director would yell, "jackets off!"

By the end of the day, my ribs were shaking quite severely, and were very sore the next day. That was probably the worst job I ever had in show business, and I made sure from then on never to expose myself to those kind of conditions on a film shoot. Some extra work I flatly refused, such as large crowd scenes and anything in painful weather conditions.

Sally was my last roommate of the 1970s, and she enjoys telling all these little stories about me. Due to the constant time changes and jet lag involved in international flying, my sleeping patterns were very irregular. One night, when it was snowing outside, I stuck my head into Sally's bedroom and asked, "Would you like a Bloody Mary?" It was three am!

She claims that she was not allowed to speak to me before I'd had my morning coffee and cigarette. This was the morning "peace period." Today, she tells me, she has become the same way.

She says I used to wear no fewer than five lipsticks to get

the right shade. I recall only three! And she still teases me about the wooden clogs I'd stomp around in at five or six in the morning, getting ready for a flight. Well, my flights always departed in the evening, so I'm not sure she got that right. I am surprised we never got complaints from the neighbors below about the noise those shoes made. As I said, the floors and walls of the building were very sturdy. I, for one, cannot stand the slightest noise from neighbors, which is one of the reasons I have moved around the city eleven times!

On one of my layovers, I bought some kind of red plastic ware. When I got home, I stashed it in the oven temporarily. You know what's coming: The oven got turned on by accident, and the item melted into what looked like a piece of twisted sculpture. We put it out as a decoration for a while and dubbed it "Bad News."

Sally insists that I accused our kindly superintendent of drinking my liquor while I was gone on a flight. I don't remember it, so perhaps she is exaggerating. I do remember that when this Irishman came to fix something in our newly painted kitchen, he looked around rather sadly and said, "What a dreadful red!"

Once, while I was standing on a stepstool attempting to hang homemade curtains, I dropped a hammer on my big toe, which began to swell and bleed. Wincing in pain, I grabbed a bottle of duty-free gin and poured it on the sore spot to ward off infection. Then I took a big swig of it. Sally found that very amusing!

Once, while I was away, a male friend of ours came over to visit and drank all the milk in the fridge. When I got home, I was so furious I left five messages on his phone. The next day he showed up with a gallon of milk and said, "After the fifth message, I thought I should bring you a *cow*."

Sally remembers that after she moved to another apartment a few blocks away, her handyman would imitate me walking around in my uniform with my "head in the air," all ponytail and attitude: "Don't you dare even *ask* me if I'm a stewardess!"

While Sally and I were waiting for a light to change at an intersection in Manhattan, this crazy bum approached me slowly and very deliberately proceeded to deposit a piece of filthy paper on top of my head. Was I a garbage dump? No, I think he thought I was a queen and needed to be crowned, the way he took a step back and looked at it with reverence! *Ah, New York.* I flipped the debris off my head, the light turned green, and we crossed—but Sally's laughter went on for blocks.

Several years later, when we were no longer roommates, Sally and I were once again waiting for a light to change. A truck driver leaned on his horn for no reason, so I looked at him with disgust. Sally claims that I cursed at him in Swedish, whereupon

Sally and me in a New York bar in the 1970s.

he rolled down his window and called out, "Oh, shut up, bitch!" "Well, you're right about that!" I snapped back. In the end, we both laughed and he gave us a thumbs-up. *Ah, New York.*

And bless the cab drivers. One driver I had pointed to an old derelict stretched out on the grassy median of Park Avenue and commented, "Look at him! He's a NU YAWKER!"

In the 1970s the city was a mess. Mr. X once remarked with sardonic humor about yet another decrepit bum, "He's an old Swede!" He loved to drive around the boroughs at top speed, and could get me to the airport in twenty minutes flat. I had never met anyone who could drive like that. It scared me at first, but I got used to it. He also owned boats, and Sally and I would sometimes cruise the New York rivers with him and another friend, Joe. Once, while on one of Mr. X's boats, we decided we wanted to shower and wash our hair. Mr. X proceeded to order us up onto a pier, then grabbed a hose and shot cold water at us. Each time he paused the stream, Sally would yell out, "I guess he believes in the 'pressure method!' He could probably shampoo an entire salon in five minutes!" We couldn't stop laughing, but Mr. X retained his usual poker face.

Once, when I got home after a grueling Tokyo trip, I was so tired that I didn't want anyone near me. Sally had invited a young man—a friend of a friend or someone's relative—over to visit. When I walked in, he greeted me pleasantly, but I took one look at him and burst out, "Fourteen hours from Tokyo!" *Get the hell out and don't talk* is what I was thinking. "Twenty minutes from Queens!" he responded politely.

After a few misfires, Sally finally found a new place to live, and soon it was my turn to move. Mr. X needed the apartment back—and eventually sold it—but not before he arranged a new rental for me with the help of our superintendent, who also took care of another building nearby. This would be Apartment Number Three, and I'd live in it for twelve years in the 1980s.

The eighties were perhaps the best decade of my life; they were certainly the most productive. New York was booming, Ronald Reagan was president, the economy was good, and the value of real estate shot up. The time seemed right for me to invest in my first house. With the guidance of Mr. X, I bought a place outside of Manhattan, rented it out for a few years, then sold it to my tenant's boyfriend for a profit. (This was fortunate for me, as she herself was on welfare and always late with the rent.) That guy probably made a killing when he sold it, as prices went through the roof in the mid-eighties. I was happy with my venture nonetheless.

Apartment Number Three was much smaller than my previous one, but it had charm. It was on the top floor of a rather small building, and had one bedroom, a living room, and a so-so kitchen and bathroom. In twelve years, I encountered only two giant water bugs and one small mouse—not bad for New York!

I visited my family quite often throughout the seventies and eighties. My father had retired as Swedish Ambassador to Ireland and he and my mother were living in a suburb of Dublin. My younger brother was there as well, studying architecture, learning dressage, and becoming a skilled horseman. My older brother and his wife Birdie were living in Sweden, and would visit Ireland every Christmas with their two sons, Carl Fredrik and Gustaf. We all got together in my parents' lovely house named Ballymadun. There was a little lane leading to it with a gate in front and meadows all around that spread out into farms. To me, Ireland was a romantic and poetic land. It suited my father, who wrote poetry and a book called *The Isle Behind the Island*, all about Ireland, as well as occasional newspaper articles for the local press.

Our family Christmas parties were something else. My widowed Aunt Ingrid loved and needed the company of my parents, so she always joined us as well. We would gather before dinner over my father's very special martinis and have real conversations—no TV! The boys would romp around and sometimes get too rowdy. Once, Gustaf BIT Carl Fredrik. My father exclaimed in Swedish, "*Som en hund!*"—like a dog! That got quite a reaction from their mother Birdie.

Today, Gustaf and Carl Fredrik are grown up and married, with two sons each, and Carl Johan, my older brother and their grandfather, will be eighty next year. My younger brother will be sixty-four, and I am not so young myself!

In 1984, our mother died at just sixty-nine years old. It was a sudden shock and took us a few years to overcome. As I have written about Mother's death previously, in the book about my father, I won't dwell on it here, nor on his a few years later, in a car accident in Malaga, Spain. I think about both my parents with all the fondness and love of a daughter—especially their sense of humor and all the precious times I spent with them.

Returning to New York in the 1980s, I think fondly about the restaurants and shopping! New York has always been an expensive town, but in those days, one could still afford the Russian Tea Room on West 57th Street. There, a whole meal with caviar and wine or Champagne went for about twenty dollars! We'd go for afternoon coffee and pastries at the Plaza, and to its famous Oak Bar for drinks. At the Grotta Azura in Little Italy, right near the place where Joey Gallo was shot, we enjoyed marvelous authentic Italian cooking. The restaurants in Chinatown offered the best Chinese food outside of Hong Kong. There was

Father and Carl Gustaf in Ireland.

also the Peking Duck House on the Upper East Side, where pieces of duck were served in a type of pancake with a tasty sauce that looked like chocolate syrup, garnished by chives or other greens. There was Forlini's, downtown near the courthouses, where all the lawyers and cops and businessmen ate their dinners, as well as the well-known Steak House on West 19th Street, another popular place for those with big appetites. By the time I finished a salad there, I had little room for the steak—but I managed to eat at least half of it because it was so good (and was, of course, followed by dessert).

Luchow's, the famous German restaurant, was one of the first places that Mr. X took me to. And, soon after I arrived in New York, someone invited me to the 21 Club, which was an experience in itself. The gentleman in question described himself as "such a New Yorker that I have concrete under my fingernails."

The shopping in New York was the best in the world in those days, particularly because of all the magnificent bargains to be had. Down on Orchard Street, I remember buying red velvet curtains for just around ten dollars. Inexpensive designer clothing was everywhere, and the quality was great! This was long before Seventh Avenue fell apart and cheap, shoddy clothing began to pour in from China and elsewhere.

Before I arrived in New York, I had never seen lacquer handbags as beautiful and affordable as those in Bloomingdales. I shopped often at Bendel's, where I also met my wonderful hair colorist, Michael Casey. He did my hair back then for forty dollars, including highlights, and I have followed him to several other locations over the years. He is like a brother.

When I was regularly going out to see photographers, casting directors, and agents, I got into the habit of taking taxi cabs all over town. The cost? Two dollars most of the time—maybe five to go to Wall Street—plus a twenty-five-cent tip. For many years, bus fare was just twenty-five-to-fifty cents so it was possible to go all over and do a million things. Today it seems to cost five dollars just to walk down the street, and at least twenty a day just to survive. Of course it's important to keep in mind that salaries in those days averaged from $20,000 to $50,000 a year; if you were making $30,000, you could live well! Rents in decent buildings ranged from $400 to $800 a month. Today? Add a zero.

Under Reagan, prices went up considerably. Forget about two-dollar cab rides, and bus fare slowly increased to a dollar. But salaries went up too, and investments increased in value, so life was still good. I remember getting seven percent interest on Money Market accounts and Certificates of Deposit. Then, all of a sudden, the stock market crashed, and it took years to recover—but we weathered it well.

At one point, Mr. X decided that, with my proficiency in languages, I should study Russian. I had an old Pan Am friend, Eva Wredenfors, who was also fluent in several languages, and together we set out to study Russian at the New School in Manhattan. Our teacher's name was Marina Federovskaya, and she was a great Russian lady in her sixties with Slavic features and grey hair piled high on her head. She confided to us once that she had hidden some contraband up there when fleeing Russia for Germany ages earlier. "Now you know my little secret," she added.

After our weekly class, we'd hijack Marina and many of our fellow classmates to one of our apartments and we'd have a great time. Besides Eva and Marina, there was a lovely Armenian woman named Julia and an assortment of others. One man whom I'll call Jim was an extremely intelligent student of mathematics. Another—call him Bruce—already spoke some Russian and seemed to belong to some sort of spy organization. I later came across him outside of a karate studio in Soho, wearing a white tunic and belt and practicing his moves.

Marina had all these ideas about people. She often spoke about the KGB, who once came knocking on her door. When

Russian class: Marina next to me in the top row; Julia and Eva in front.

Susan's collage of me.

someone asked her how she knew it was the KGB, she replied in her inimitable Russian accent, "Who eeeeeelse?"

Along with all the fun, I did learn some Russian, but to really learn a language properly, you have to speak it every day—preferably in its country of origin. So, in addition to our studies, we spent a lot of time socializing—to the dismay of Jim the mathematician, who was there for serious study. The "spy" guy, Bruce, did not seem to care as much, so I wondered what he was really doing there.

"Girrls, girrls, I tell you sooomething!" Marina would say in her funny accent. She would talk a lot about Faberge Eggs and drinking Dubonnet. She described the locals in Germany, where she had lived for a while, as very duty-bound with their "*putsen und sparen*"—cleaning and saving. She pronounced Eva's name "*Jeva*," I was "*Ami*," and Julia was "*Hulia*." We all loved Marina but eventually the sessions stopped and we all went on our merry ways.

Sadly, I've forgotten all the Russian I learned. *Ja ni pomnio Russki Yasik.* But I will always remember the beautiful Russian song my father used to sing, "*Gaida Troika, Snieg Poshisti, Noch Marosnaya Grogom.*" I've probably gotten some of the letters wrong, but it's about a troika (three-horse sleigh) gliding over the glittering snow on a dark and star-studded night, and it's very romantic. I look back on the decades of the seventies and eighties as the most rewarding times of my life, for three reasons (in addition to the city itself): show business, Pan Am, and Mr. X!

Chapter Sixteen

Changing Altitude

1990s NEW YORK

On December 4, 1991, Pan American World Airways was grounded for good. The greatest airline ever was no more. It had survived a lot, but after the Lockerbie terrorist incident, bookings fell off by eighteen percent, and that was on top of the fact that people were already fearful due to previous attacks. These included hijackings in Caracas and Cairo, a bomb on the tarmac in Rome and one under a seat in San Francisco, and the storming by Hezbollah of a 747 in Karachi. Poor management and lack of domestic routes were the other two nails in the Pan Am coffin.

Delta Airlines entered our lives, having acquired most of Pan Am rather cheaply. They hired many of us but let others go. There were lawsuits, and that is another story. My own interview with Delta went quite well. I was hired for my language skills—which Delta sorely needed—and for my twenty-six years of experience and status as a Purser. My main concern was that I be allowed to continue pursuing my second career—show business—between flights, but my new employer had fewer objections to this than Pan Am had.

It was definitely a different culture. Delta is a southern airline headquartered in Atlanta, which, at the time, ran mostly domestic routes though it now flies all over the world. There is no doubt that it is a very successful enterprise, but for me, the thrill was gone forever. I was a Pan Am-er, and although I was grateful to Delta for hiring me, I knew my life would never be the same. Delta was a *job* whereas Pan Am had been a *lifestyle*. For me, that was that.

Still based in New York, I was now only flying to Europe. Although it was my least favorite destination, I did enjoy Eastern Europe—Budapest, Warsaw, Helsinki, and my native Stockholm, where I had family. I also flew to Moscow, and was once interviewed and photographed for a magazine there. The result was a very long article about my feelings and attitudes toward the flying profession. My picture was unsmiling and very Russian—as opposed to the friendly shots of crew members in American publications. "She likes to swim with dolphins," read one of the sentences in the article. I have no idea where that came from. The article was translated from Russian to English for me by my friend and fellow Russian student Eva Wredenfors, who spoke five languages fluently. My name had been changed to Ann Peyt . . . for security reasons?

One year before Pan Am folded, I acquired my first co-op apartment in the city. It was my third real estate venture, after the house outside Manhattan and a small studio in Stockholm I'd inherited from my mother. I'd intended to use the Stockholm place as a pied-à-terre, but ended up selling it quickly for a nice profit because of the currency fluctuation. Amazingly, the Swedish tax authorities sent back the tax I paid on it, which was not so much, but still a surprise. I did have to declare the profit in the U.S., of course, but that didn't result in a large bill either.

So now I faced an interview by the board of my first co-op in the city, in Murray Hill. Anyone who has been through this knows what a nerve-wracking ordeal it is to purchase a co-op. First, you have to assemble every document you can imagine, then go through the process of securing a mortgage—which can take three to six months—and then comes the board interview, during which strangers delve into both your finances and personal life. Are you a responsible individual, able to pay your maintenance, even if you lose your job or get sued? On the basis of your answers, you are either accepted or crushed. My interview in front of six members of the board went okay. After I left and was standing in the lobby, I could hear someone saying, "Well...."

I was accepted and the day of the big move came. I remember walking a few blocks in the snow with Mr. X to get there. The place was on the seventeenth floor, a one bedroom with a big eat-in kitchen and a large terrace facing east. The price had certainly been right. In 1991 the market was depressed so I got lucky. Ten years later, when I sold it, the unit's value had gone up fifty percent! This was apartment Number Four, and I named it the "Castle in the Sky." Every place I lived got a name—all eleven of them!

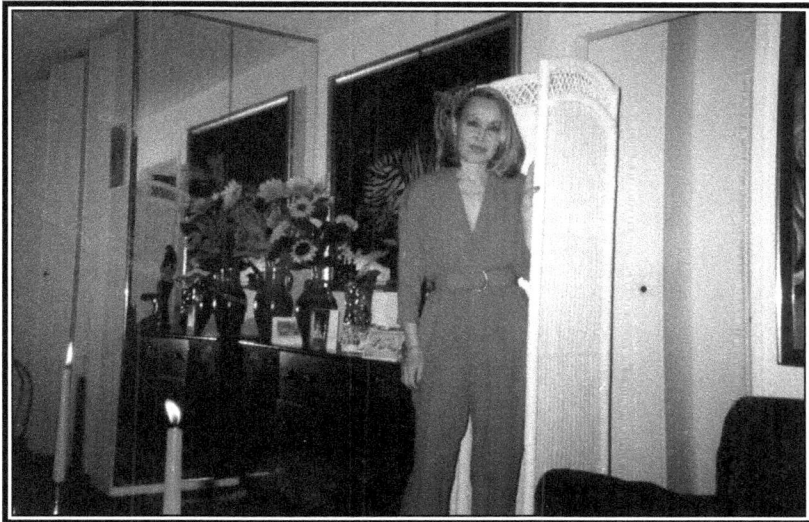

Hostess of the "Castle in the Sky."

Aunt Ingrid, c. 1940.

After I sold the Stockholm studio, I got a new idea about Sweden. I was quite gung-ho about apartments, and still wanted a pied-à-terre in my native country. My aunt Ingrid was living in Malmö, the third largest city in Sweden, in the South. She was a widow and very much missed my mother—with whom she'd been very close—so she was always happy to see me and the rest of the family. She sometimes went on tourist excursions to Mallorca and other places, and once she met an older gentleman, a widower. They were together for a few years, but then he died also. After that, I remember her saying to me, "And now I have *nobody*!"

I decided to buy a very small one-roomer, as we called it, in a building next to Aunt Ingrid's. I figured I could rent it out when I wasn't using it—but it turned out that wasn't permitted. I got it for $20,000, which seemed like a good price at the time, but in fact, I was taken advantage of. When I went to sell it a few years later, I found that it was not worth more than $5,000. Still, I got lucky—sort of. The lady below me wanted to combine units and bought it for $10,000. The deal was settled in an hour, at a bank, with two pieces of paper. Compare that to Manhattan where, mortgage or not, seemingly hundreds of documents are required, along with a million copies of each one!

My Malmö adventure was fun in spite of my loss, but I visited Sweden only rarely and never intended to live there. Aunt Ingrid understood when I decided to give it up. I reassured her that I could always fly over and see her, and I did.

During the last decade of her life, Aunt Ingrid became more and more eccentric and difficult to get along with. Once, when she visited her half-brother, Eric Robbert, in Greece, she arrived with a bottle of Scotch as a gift. After some kind of quarrel between them, she demanded money for it. Eric had to go and borrow from a neighbor! Ingrid needed constant attention and was forever getting into combative arguments. It's a shame that she turned out that way, but I will always remember her as my glamorous Aunt Ingrid.

In her heyday, Ingrid was a model in New York, celebrated and courted by many prominent men. She never really cared for them, though, or marriage for that matter. She did marry a nice businessman named Bengt and they were together for twelve years, until he died of liver damage. "This thing with *relationships,*" she once commented, "it's a difficult thing!" (Her words may carry more weight in Swedish: "*Det är svårt, det där med förhållanden!*") This reminds me of something the great dramatist August Strindberg once said: "*Det är SYND om människorna!*" which is usually interpreted as, "I feel sorry for people!" But really what he meant should probably be interpreted as, "I feel for mankind," or something like that.

There is a story about Ingrid that is quite amazing. In the late thirties, when Hitler was at the height of his power, one of many parades was held in a German city in his honor. Ingrid happened to be visiting at the time. Tall and blond and wearing a white dress and large-brimmed hat, she stood out among the crowd, watching. As Hitler approached, Ingrid did not perform the "Heil" gesture—why would she?

As the story goes, Hitler stopped the parade! According to my aunt, he walked right over to her and bored his steel-grey eyes into hers. He raised his arm in the Nazi salute. Shocked beyond belief, Ingrid managed to raise her hand halfheartedly, then bow her head a tad. The parade continued, but afterwards, members of the Gestapo approached her and began to ask questions. "*Ich bin ja nur eine turiste!*" she replied—I'm only a tourist!

Aunt Ingrid died in 1998, and I think of her every day. I only hope I can manage not to become eccentric!

I love all kinds of animals—cats, dogs, horses—and I have a lot of animal stories from the 1990s. But let me lead into one of them by telling you about a dear friend.

My friend Christina, whom I've known since the seventies, is more like a sister. She is very Swedish, but has the drive, energy, and *joie de vivre* of a successful American. She has had a million jobs and is a bit of a nomad, having lived in Sweden,

New York, and Florida, among other places. To this day, Christina crosses the Atlantic the way some people cross the street. She has two loveable sons and a husband named Ragnar, a very kindly and tolerant Swede who puts up with all her benign caprices. She is by far the most positive Swedish person I have ever known—another way in which she is like an American. A positive spirit, and can-do attitude are not endemic to most places—certainly not to Sweden.

In the early seventies, Christina ran all over Manhattan selling skirts for a women's wear company. You could spot her on the sidewalk, burdened down with up to ten skirts, calling on

Christina, Annie, and me in Florida.

potential buyers. She had long, curly, blond hair, and the skirts were wide and colorful, so she was quite noticeable—and did very well. That job was followed by a wide variety of others, mostly in fashion and cosmetics, always on the sales side.

Now, we get to the animal story. Christina had a cat named Rufus, and at one point, when she had to run off to Sweden for some reason, she asked if I could take care of him. It was supposed to be for a few months, but ended up being nine! Rufus was a New York tabby who looked like a tiger and was very naughty. He would laze around with his ample stomach hanging out—I never saw a cat with such a big personality.

Rufus would wake me up at three in the morning by jumping onto my bed and staring at me intently until I got up to feed him. He was a big pain in the posterior, but I loved him.

Then there is the story of Arnold. One day, I saw this forlorn little black dog on the sidewalk, tied to a pole. I knew

Arnold and me.

right away that something was wrong. He looked abandoned, and someone told me he had been there for two hours. I bent over him and sure enough I found a note under his collar that read, "Please adopt me. I can be a bit difficult to handle, but I really am a good dog."

A small crowd gathered as I tried to decide what to do. "Poor little thing," said a young man. "Someone just left him there!" He and I decided to take the little dog to the Bide-a Wee down the street. The young man left right away and there I stood with Arnold, as we decided to call him.

What was I going to do with him? I knew I couldn't keep him because I had recently joined Delta and would be away a lot. On top of that, I was adjusting to the culture of a new airline and undergoing what I felt were bizarre training sessions and indoctrination.

I called Sally on the phone, and she promptly came down to the Bide-a-Wee. The vet had just examined Arnold, and he was a very nervous little dog. To make a long story short, Sally opened her heart and adopted Arnold. I felt bad that I couldn't help her with him very much, but I did walk him now and then.

There was no petting Arnold—he wouldn't allow it. Maybe he'd been abused, or maybe he was just a mental case. He was a soulful little dog, though, and we shared many humorous moments because of his personality.

I had moved to my fifth apartment by then, a temporary one after I sold the Castle in the Sky. I called this one the Little Hovel. It was a tiny rental on the seventeenth floor of a building in the same neighborhood, but it had no view at all and was quite dark. When Sally and Arnold came to visit, it was clear that he was not impressed. After a few minutes, he adopted a funny expression, as if he were politely trying to say, "Let's get the hell out of here!" I really think he was trying to be patient and polite! Arnold wasn't wrong. Soon enough, I wanted to get the hell out of there, too, having set my sights on a co-op apartment on Park Avenue nearby.

Sally had Arnold for ten years, and when he passed away from an illness it was one of the saddest days of our lives. We loved that dog, and I wrote a little poem for him in tribute.

Ode to the Little Darling

I found you in the street, abandoned, eyes wandering, tied
    to a pole.
How could I just walk by a little creature so sweet!
How would I guess, you'd play the role,
ten years of the most beloved pet,
to your Mommy Sally and Auntie me.
I promptly took you to the vet,
That's where Sally and you met.
Those black eyes, how could one resist,
A little chubby body, short legs and cute feet.
But you would bark and bark, you did insist
 Until you got that morsel treat.
A little old man you looked like, we used to say
Arnold, Arnold became you name
Most of the time you got your way
in Murray Hill you soon had fame!
Ten years of endless love you gave and got
Not only will we miss you a lot
Such a soulful dog there was not!
This was Arnold, yes indeed
Where are you now, where did you go?
My little darling, there is still the need
Can't help feeling so low!
Thinking of you I hope you're at peace

We loved you so,
Only that gives my mind a little ease.
Rest well my sweet
Some time we'll meet. . . .

I ended up selling the Castle in the Sky to my next-door neighbors, who wanted to expand their space. After a lengthy ordeal with a bank, they were happy and so was I, with my substantial profit. I lived in the Little Hovel for just a year only before I bought the co-op on Park Avenue—my second one.

My job flying for Delta turned into what I called semi-retirement. It was a new kind of flying for me—short hops, easy as pie! No more international flying; I'd had to put a stop to it because the constant time changes were giving me migraines. I think my last flight to Europe was to Brussels, and I never went back.

I was quite happy bidding on brief continuations of flights that had originated in Europe, stopped at JFK, and would go on to such destinations as Philadelphia, Boston, and Washington. I'd report for one of these mini-flights at two pm and be home by six, with just half an hour in the air each way, no service to speak of—only announcements—and *very good pay*.

The century had come to its end and the thrill was gone, as the song goes. But there would still be many highlights to follow. New York was changing. It was far less dirty and crime-ridden, and foreigners were moving in in droves, from all over the world. The prices, though—the cost of everything was going through the roof, and it seemed that none of the good restaurants were affordable anymore. Shopping was much more expensive too, and bargains were hard to find. The Seventh Avenue fashion district was disappearing right along with phone booths and cozy little coffee shops. Instead, there was a Starbucks on every corner and a million electronics stores.

Manhattan was fast becoming gentrified: a playground for the rich. Don't get me wrong—it was still a great city and still is today—but its former character began to erode, a process that has continued.

So there I was, in 2001, having moved to Park Avenue. Little did I know what was coming. The *big blow*. The *catastrophe*.

Chapter Seventeen

Park Avenue on the Roof

2001 NEW YORK

The move from the Little Hovel to Park Avenue and 34th Street was a dream come true. The real estate agent who had shown me the studio on the fifteenth floor was not exactly the most professional, and I had to handle a lot of the paperwork on my own—but I managed to get the place at a pretty good price from an older couple who were motivated to sell. This was April 2001, and the market was still affordable.

My lawyer was better than my broker, and helped me navigate my way toward the board interview. I made ten copies of all the paperwork the board required and had it delivered to each board member individually. Finally the date for the interview was set.

Not wanting to spend another night in the Little Hovel, I was nervous about the interview. These things usually take place in small rooms off the lobby areas of the co-ops. This one was not what I expected. Although there were six board members, the interview was conducted by just one lady. "Pan Am hired only *blondes*, right?" she asked sardonically—the nerve! Here I was desperately hoping to acquire a desirable apartment and she was being snide! "They hired women from South America also!" I commented, keeping my temper in check. The subject changed to my finances, and I had to point out an important detail she'd overlooked. Anyway, it all ended well.

Ricardo.

I moved my belongings, which did not amount to much thanks to my frequent moves, into Apartment Number Six—my exclusive little studio on Park, with a great view of the Empire State Building. The building was old but wonderful and had a communal terrace on the top floor, the twenty-fourth, with 360-degree views of the city below. This terrace would become a popular gathering place for me and my fellow residents, who, like the population of New York as a whole, ran the gamut of types. Most were working people with jobs on Wall Street, in the garment district, in publishing and media, or as graphic designers or photographers. My next-door neighbor Ricardo became a close friend and remains one to this day. He is a tall, very good looking man from Argentina who works as a tour guide all over the U.S.A., and for a while, he had a business selling empanadas. He plays the piano and has other talents as well. He is the warmest and most sympathetic person, and accompanied me to the hospital once, when I needed someone. He even let me stay in his apartment from time to time, after I moved away from Park Avenue and was having noise problems in my new place. Ricardo is a most loveable human being!

Another neighbor on Park was Susan, the "mystery lady." Susan was very flamboyant and glamorous, with a background she preferred to keep obscure. If you asked her any specific questions about her life, you got vague answers as she looked off into space. I did learn that she was a native New Yorker, raised in Brooklyn, and that she had eloped with a man—I believe it was to France. None of her stories really made sense. For instance, it turned out that her sixteenth-floor apartment belonged to someone else, but she'd made us believe it was hers. She claimed she had been abused by some man, but the details were sketchy.

Susan.

Poor Susan. She had no family and very few friends. Ricardo and I got to know her quite well as we sunbathed together on the roof in our bikinis. Being a brazen sort, and something of an exhibitionist, Susan would remove her top halfway. She loved to talk politics, had a million opinions about everything, and yes, she was very eloquent, using words like "conundrum." Her favorite phrase for people's obsession with handheld devices was, "electronic masturbation!"

Like all New Yorkers, Susan had a sense of humor—but she would descend into vulnerable moods, getting upset over inconsequential things. She and I might have a phone conversation, then she'd follow it up with two or three calls to clarify "What did I mean by that?" Something innocuous I'd said had hurt her, so I'd have to explain myself and set her mind at ease. It was exhausting and draining.

She did do a lovely thing for me, though, that took some skill. She assembled an assortment of my modeling pictures, movie shots, and movie posters into an attractive collage. I had copies made, then framed the original, which still hangs on my wall. In return for her kindness, I had an illustration made and framed, based on a photo of her boyfriend who had died shortly after I moved into the building. She missed him terribly and talked about him nonstop. She deeply appreciated the gesture.

Susan was one of a kind—like someone out of a novel. Eventually, she was evicted from her apartment and Ricardo and I lost touch with her. She did call me a few times, from various numbers, but never disclosed where she was living. She would be in her late seventies now. She smoked three packs of cigarettes a day, so I have to wonder if she's still alive. Lately, a number of my former colleagues and friends have passed away very suddenly at that age. I find myself at a strange time in my life, when these events happen. Life isn't the same anymore. People and places are here today, gone tomorrow!

We called Apartment Number Six the Opium Den, and I decorated it with red velvet curtains, a sofa and pillows of mixed materials and fabrics, and an oriental carpet. There were two walk-in closets, and it was possible to sit in the windowed kitchen if you were skinny enough to perch on a high stool by a mini table. We threw a few Christmas parties at the Opium Den, and Susan insisted upon giving us all presents she'd wrapped in colorful silky paper, tied with elaborate bows. "It has to be festive," she'd say.

An old Pan Am friend visited a few times; it was actually she who came up with the name for the place, or I might have dubbed it the Little Bordello.

You must think all my apartments were little—just wait. Another old friend, a banker I'll call Joe, arranged one mortgage after another for me, as well as "cash-out refinance," a great way to benefit from the equity in one's apartment, when it goes up in value. New York real estate is a wonder, and UP it went in the early 2000s. In fact, between 2000 and 2006, it went through the roof. My apartment almost tripled in value during those years, and the time came to sell again.

But that was all after the big catastrophe. On September 11, 2001, Susan and I were hanging around and socializing up on the roof, as usual. One thing we were discussing was the news I'd heard earlier that morning, about an airplane crash at the Pentagon. I immediately suspected terrorism, because in the airline business we were always thinking along those lines. Osama Bin Laden had been a threat for quite a while, and since the Pan Am days—and especially after the Lockerbie incident—I, for one, had been annoyed at the public's ignorance of this global situation. I believed that the FBI and CIA were not focusing enough energy and attention on airline security. I remember one colleague at Delta making a comment around New Year's, 2001, to the effect, "What if Osama Bin Laden were to strike now?" The response was total denial.

The view from the Park Avenue rooftop.

Make no mistake (and I have already touched on this): we were experiencing acts of terrorism in the early seventies, and perhaps as early as the sixties. In those days, it was hijackings, mostly. Many people think that the events of 9/11 were the first significant incident. Not so.

From our rooftop, Susan and I couldn't see what was

Lounging on the roof.

unfolding in Lower Manhattan, but we could detect a faint smell of smoke. Very soon, we learned the unspeakable truth about the World Trade towers. There had been four terrorist crashes in all, involving American and United Air Lines planes. These were coast-to-coast flights, the kind I often flew for Delta at them time. They could easily have been Delta flights.

The city has recovered, but it has never really been the same since. The hustle and bustle and energy and aggression characteristic of New York died down considerably for a long time. It was as if a veil had been drawn over the city. Everything slowed to a trickle, and the atmosphere was somber. Unfamiliar.

A few years later, I decided to become an American citizen. It seemed like a good idea for security reasons, and since I'd lived here for forty years, it was about time. I'd always felt like a citizen, and my Green Card had paved the way with no problems. But I went through the required procedures and waited for about a year. In 2003, I became a U.S. citizen, end of story.

By this point, I had also had had my fill of flying. The job was not particularly rewarding anymore, nor was it any fun. Delta abruptly ended those short Philadelphia hops, so I'd been doing some easy Cincinnati turnarounds—but when those ended, I was stuck with Atlanta turns. There was no way I'd go back to overseas flying, what with my migraines, the time changes, and the grueling hours.

The Golden Age of Aviation was long gone, and I wasn't the only one who missed Pan Am—ask anyone who worked for them. And speaking of old, I was becoming too old to fly! Along with the migraines, I was starting to develop serious eye diseases and vertigo. On one of my last Delta flights to Atlanta, working in the First Class cabin, I experienced severe floaters and flashes in my left eye. To make matters worse, there was a rather intolerant Delta supervisor on board with whom I had issues. That

was the last straw. I decided to accept a so-so "early out" the following year. It was not such a great deal they were offering, but
I was ready. In January 2005, I said goodbye to Delta Air Lines.

After almost forty years of flying, twenty-six with Pan Am
and thirteen with Delta, it was the right move. The thrill, enjoyment, and adventure were long gone. The job had become
oppressive. My final position with Delta was as an Inflight
Coordinator, a position without much authority but with loads
of responsibilities. In contrast, I look back on my Pan Am years
as one big party, in spite of the company's troubles at the end
and inevitable demise. Delta remains a successful airline, but I
have faced the fact that I never quite belonged there.

Sadly, the pension I now receive is pocket money, thanks
to something called "Social Security Offset." Delta took away
sixty-five percent of my pension at age sixty-two, based on the
idea that I was then eligible to collect Social Security. Not very
Christian of them, but that's what happens when you have no
union to negotiate for you.

I did much better in my retirement from show business.
As a member of the Screen Actors Guild (now called SAG
AFTRA), I receive excellent secondary medical insurance in
addition to a small pension. You needed ten credits to qualify
for the Senior Plan and I have twelve. As I detail earlier in this
book, and in *The Other Side of Stardom,* I worked with such
directors as Woody Allen, Alan Pakula, and Martin Scorsese
in such films as *Raging Bull, Presumed Innocent, Still of the
Night, Arthur, All that Jazz,* and *Baby Boom.*

In spite of the long and tedious hours, my experiences in
the business have left me with great memories as well as mon-
etary benefits. When my old friend Penny passed away
recently, I thought back about all the great jobs we did
together, along with her friend, Richard du Bois. Penny's

feisty mother lived to be 103, and always referred to Richard as *that Richard*. Besides being an actor, Richard assisted with the cleanup of Ground Zero after 9/11. Bravo, man!

I've written a lot about the casting director Sylvia Fay, also prominent in my memories. Also important to me were Grant Wilfley and Joy Todd, who cast me in many films in which I got upgrades and silent bits. I worked with Barbara Claman for TV commercials and Louis di Giamo, who cast *The Godfather*. Wonderful photographers came into my life, including Valentin, who shot glamorous pictures of me in the 1970s, and Jimmy Kriegsman, who took my headshots. I met and worked with so many others, but it was all a long time ago and everything has to come to an end.

My very last job in show business was in 2009, doing background work in *Black Swan*. The scene was beautiful, featuring an upscale black, white, and silver wardrobe of floor-length dresses and black tie. The idea was to create the perfect background for the white silk tutu of the ballerina star. It was a late night shoot in downtown New York, and I realized that long hours on sets were starting to get the best of me. These shoots could go on for ten to twenty hours—for which we'd get paid what was called "golden time"—and would sometimes begin at four am!

After *Black Swan*, I never accepted another booking. Although I was done with show business, I have no regrets about my four decades of work—not even the freezing cold or unbearable heat. It was all such a lark between flights in my sometimes petty and ultra-conservative airline milieu. My two occupations complemented each other well for forty years, and then it was over.

In 2006, the time came for me to move again. My Park Avenue studio was very lovely, but I was developing an intense intolerance for the noise above me. My reaction was akin to claustrophobia. Some people are not bothered at all by noise around them, and even I can tolerate New York sirens, traffic, and construction. But if someone next door or above is playing music or walking around with shoes on, my blood pressure rises, my nerves take a hit, and I have to get out.

In my place on Park, I was constantly bombarded from above by the sounds of kids romping around and what sounded like furniture being moved. I left notes under the tenants' door, only to be accosted with a knock on my door and a nasty visit. "Had I heard of lawyers?" they asked me. Ah yes, New York!

There is a rule within co-ops that carpeting must cover eighty percent of the floor, but it is not strictly enforced. Lucky for me, it was once again a sellers' market and I knew I could make a good sale if I wanted to. It didn't take me long to decide: Get away from these noisy neighbors and pocket a nice cash profit.

So the little Opium Den was sold in 2006 by a very formidable real estate agent named Cheryl, who happened to live in

Penny and Richard.

the building. I got triple what I had paid for it, thanks to her. And then, there I was: no home, no job, but some money and some friends.

There was this friend of ours, Mr. X and I, with whom we had entered into a sort of business venture in the late eighties, flying back and forth to Europe where the selling of some goods was done. There is no need to go into detail because I was not really part of it, but my free tickets on Pan Am included benefits for family. It was decided that this friend—I'll call him Arthur—and I would marry so he could fly on Pan Am for free, and the three of us would benefit from this overseas business. I had my doubts about this "marriage" idea, and promptly had a pre-nuptial agreement drawn up to protect myself. It may sound a bit crazy, but it was all legitimate. Flying had its perks, and why not take advantage of them? Anyway, it lasted for a few years, then ended abruptly in an amicable yet rather bizarre divorce.

So, when I sold the Park Avenue place, I decided to plant myself at Arthur's for a while, in his Upper East Side rental apartment. He'd gotten all those free flights, after all, so he owed me. Call this Apartment Number Seven, and call it awful! It came in very handy though.

Arthur was living in Europe, so I had his huge place to myself—three bedrooms, three bathrooms, and a very large living room and kitchen, on the third floor overlooking Third Avenue. So, what was so bad about it? The aura hanging over it, due to Arthur's constant court battles with the building's owner. There were constant threats of eviction, lawsuits back and forth…again, ah, New York!

On top of that, Arthur's children had a habit of showing up and making a pigsty of the place the likes of which I have never seen. They were nice, sweet kids, but I had to wonder about their upbringing. Arthur and I were still friends, but

Mr. X was out of the picture—another story altogether.

The arrangement was that I would live there on my own, in style and comfort, but forget that! Arthur would drop in unexpectedly—a situation I didn't appreciate at all. The whole arrangement lasted only three months, and I now think of the place as one of my "parking spaces," large, somber, awkward, and filled with very negative vibes!

I was bound to end up back in Midtown. I managed to get a desirable little rental in a new area for me, Tudor City, a secluded little secret enclave close to Murray Hill. It's a beautiful complex of ten or so buildings stretching between 41st and 43rd Streets, close to the East River, the United Nations, and the Chrysler Building. It was built in 1929 in the Tudor Style, featuring arches, the Tudor lily, and plenty of gargoyles and other stone sculptures. In the middle are two wonderful parks with steps leading up to the three main buildings.

Most of the units in Tudor City are very small studios, although some have been combined into bigger apartments. I settled into a little rental in Building Number Five, on the twentieth floor with a fantastic view of the boats traveling down the East River. This was meant to be yet another "parking space" for me, but would end up being my home for four years. Of course it had a name right away: the View with a Room." I called it this because the *view* was big while the *room* was little! In spite of its size, the place was so convenient that I was very comfortable there. Tudor City is a wonderful place to live, and the parks make it very special. I have remained there to this day, though not in the View with a Room!

In 2010 it was time to buy again. Let's just say that the "Great Big Witch on the Hudson" was starting to change for me, in

A stone lion on the roof of Tudor City.

a way I can only describe as "From Sizzle to Fizzle."

I now had three authored books to my credit. *Glamour and Turbulence: I Remember Pan Am* has sold a remarkable 15,000 copies (plus any number of pirated ones) since it was published in 1996, and is still selling online. My second book,

The view from the "View with a Room."

a memoir about my showbiz experiences in New York, has never sold as well as the Pan Am book, but is still my favorite. The third book, *Diplomat, Poet, Gentleman: My Father* is perhaps the most exclusive, and tells the story of my father and the diplomatic posts where he served.

I am lucky to be able to continue to fly all over at a discount, and attend Airline Memorabilia shows where I sign and sell all of my books. Between that and my Amazon sales, I guess you could call me an author by trade at this point, an activity which has kept me quite busy in my retirement years. "From Sizzle to Fizzle" is meant to describe the still active but more sedate kind of living I do now, as a writer.

Chapter Eighteen

From Sizzle to Fizzle

2010s NEW YORK

From the rooftop of one of the Tudor City buildings where I liked to sunbathe in the summer, I could see the beautiful thirty-two-story Woodstock building, built in 1929. It recedes at the top like a wedding cake, with parapets descending to the fourteenth floor, and the Gothic look of it held an attraction for me. In Swedish we would refer to it as *Kråkslott*—castle of crows. It cuts an eerie and romantic image.

At the time, I was habitually searching the *New York Times* real estate section for studios to buy in Tudor City. Suddenly, there it was: a one-bedroom on the twenty-sixth floor of the Woodstock Tower, for the quite reasonable price of $375,000. Well, it turned out to be a studio that, with some imagination, could be converted into a one bedroom with the use of a partition. It had a renovated "Pullman kitchen," which suited me fine, but also a Murphy bed, which was not to my taste. I would eventually have it removed and replaced with a regular bed.

I contacted the broker, a very capable Indian lady with the Bellmarc Agency, who promptly declared the apartment mine, though several others were bidding on this attractive unit in a desirable location. After a lot of wrangling, and with the assistance of yet another real estate agent named Sherrie, I scored.

The seller and I signed the contract in 2010. My lawyer was contacted, and once again, I anticipated the make-or-

Carl Johan.

break board interview. This one turned out to be a breeze. A mild-mannered young woman asked me a few questions and that was it. I was all set to move into Apartment Number Nine, my third co-op in the city.

Goodbye, View with a Room and hello, Apartment 2609: the Jewel. From the main window of the Jewel, I could look across 42nd Street to the beautiful Chrysler Building. Through the East-facing windows, I could see the 59th Street Bridge, the United Nations, and the East River. The Jewel was especially beautiful at night, when all of those landmarks were illuminated until they sparkled like diamonds.

I moved in quickly and, as always, pared down my belongings even further. I am the exact opposite of a "bag lady" or hoarder, throwing everything away or selling it. There used to be an auction place on 27th Street where I could unload artifacts, oriental carpets, and other mementos collected over my years of flying for Pan Am. It was very convenient for me, and I sold a lot. The last item I sold, before all of this kind of business migrated online, was a Swedish Rya rug in a rather obscure auction shop all the way down by the Hudson River. For me, the Internet is too much of a hassle.

As 2012 drew to a close, it was time for me to visit my native country. I flew over for Christmas for about a week and finally got to be with both of my brothers at the same time. I stayed in a hotel near my younger brother because his apartment in southern Stockholm was a bit crowded. His good friend and partner Ulf, one of the most sympathetic people I have ever met, was staying with him.

Carl Johan, my older brother, came to visit on Christmas Eve, which is when Swedish people celebrate the holiday with an elaborate Christmas dinner, exchange of gifts, and more. It

Carl Gustaf.

was a very white Christmas. The snow was a yard high and the weather was crispy cold, maybe minus-twenty degrees Centigrade, and the sky was glittering with stars.

That was eight years ago and I really don't know when I will return. Sweden has changed, I hear, and I don't know if I belong there anymore or how I would adapt after fifty-four years in the United States. As I noted earlier, although it is my native country, I have spent just a total of nine years there, and that was a long time ago!

One thing is certain, I will remain in the States as long as I have my Mr. X. I haven't offered many stories about him, as I think most love relationships should remain private. The details are only interesting to the partners themselves, and the complexities are really their business, nobody else's. Let's leave it at this: Mr. X is someone I have known for fifty years—a long time—and have almost daily contact with.

Lois.

The center of Stockholm.

Over the course of that same holiday period in 2012, I visited my California family: my Aunt Lois and Uncle Carl (my mother's brother) and my cousins Anna Lisa and Ingrid. My third cousin, Bengt, was there as well. He is a vagabond of sorts, an individualist who answers to no one—a bit of a black sheep—but I like him. We had a great party, an elaborate evening with an orchestra and a special bar. Lots of neighbors came and we danced, something I had not done in a while. As I write this, Aunt Lois and Uncle Carl are no longer with us, but all those birthday parties that Lois arranged for Carl remain highlights of my time with my Swedish-American family.

Aunt Lois was the one who inspired me to write, saying, "Why don't you make up a story about an affair with a pilot!" She was highly educated, with a background in journalism and several admired books to her name. I thought her idea was a nonstarter, but I did embark on the account of my experiences with Pan Am.

Uncle Carl was ninety-two when he passed away, an American success story who arrived in the States with his motorbike in his twenties and became a well-to-do businessman in California. He married Lois, had three children, and retired in Corona del Mar, a beautiful seaside town. I visited the family there and Lois made a celebration for my fiftieth birthday. These are memories that mean something to me. Now, both

The cousins.

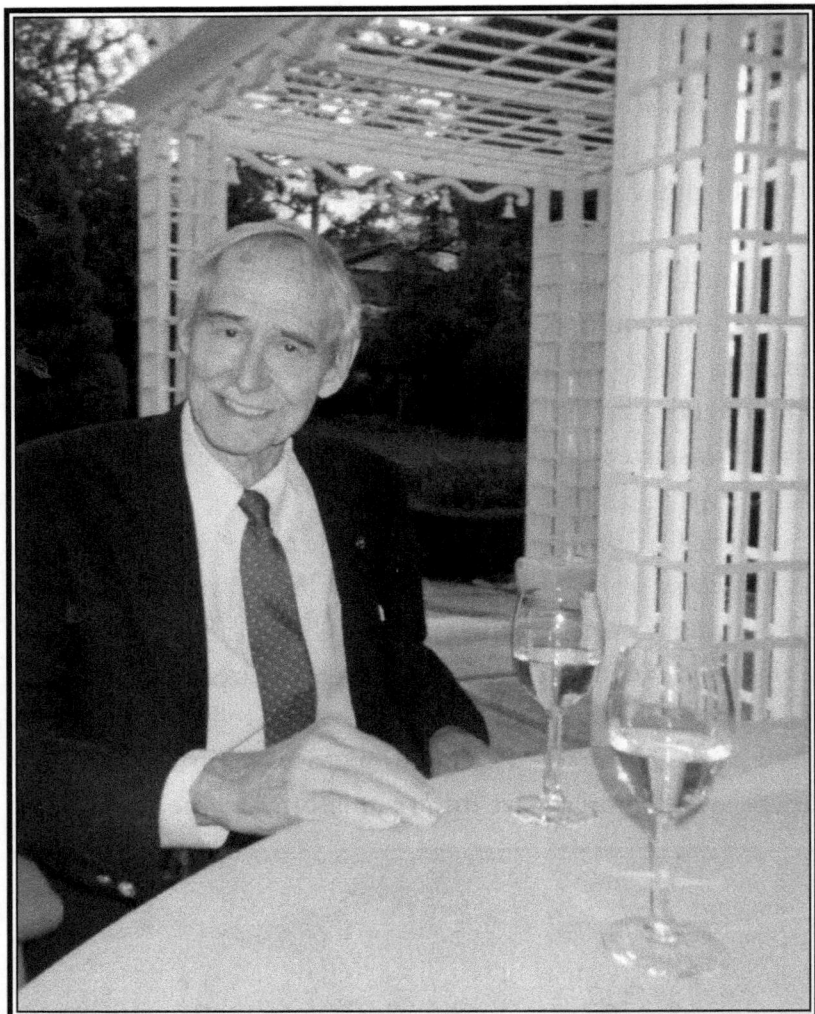

Uncle Carl, looking good at age ninety.

Anna Lisa, married to Victor, a Cuban American, and Ingrid live in the San Francisco area and are doing very well.

I refer to the year 2013 as my *Annus Horribilis.* I was developing serious eye problems. Anyone afflicted with the effects of detached retinas and severe macular degeneration will certainly understand how frightening and unpleasant these experiences can be.

These issues had begun to present themselves while I was living on Park Avenue. I was coming down in the elevator one day, after lounging in the sun on the roof, when a black streak appeared across the field of vision in my left eye. I tried to rub it away—to no avail. At the time, I was still flying for Delta, so I called a special on-duty nurse who told me to go to the emergency room at the nearest hospital.

I dashed over to NYU Hospital, where I waited for many hours. Finally, a doctor examined me and mentioned something about "drusen" in the retina. She explained that I had a detached vitreous and referred me to an eye doctor, who did nothing for me during my visit with him.

The next day, I saw my primary care doctor, who referred me to a retina specialist at a place on the Upper East Side called Retina Macula Vitreous Specialists of New York. That's when things started moving. It was there that I would meet Dr. Richard Spaide, who would eventually save my eyesight.

On my first visit, though, I was examined by a very nice doctor who looked a bit like a New York detective on *Law and Order*. He discovered a hole or tear in my retina and treated it with a laser, right there in the office.

No luck. I still saw the black streak. It was on my next visit that I met Dr. Spaide, who found yet another hole and lasered my eye a second time. The experience can be a bit shocking, with all of these psychedelic lights bombarding your eye—yellow, purple, blue, and green. The bill was shocking, too: $3,000! At the time, Dr. Spaide was not taking Medicare, but I was not informed of that beforehand. After some wrangling, I got the money back and today, thank God, he does take Medicare. At the time, I had to switch to another doctor who took my insurance.

The black streak remained, but dissolved into a kind of shadow that was tolerable. Meanwhile, my right eye developed a problem of its own—a sort of "golden field" that I noticed particularly at night. It was the beginning of a detached retina! Flashes and floaters should be examined right away by specialists. They can be relatively harmless but if they are large or numerous there could be detachment. This new eye surgeon who took Medicare (and, by the way, possessed movie-star looks) immediately declared my problem an emergency and scheduled surgery for the following evening at nine. The whole thing took only about twenty minutes, and a very considerate former colleague named Helga, now a neighbor in the Woodstock Tower, picked me up at the hospital.

Afterwards, I found that I was seeing a kind of moveable edge within my field of vision, and a very disturbing bright light and a kind of glittering, even with my eyes closed. It was like looking at a beach with moving ocean water and a sky above. I wondered how I would sleep! But the image did dissipate somewhat, and I managed.

I was told that these operations have a success rate of about eighty percent. Well, the next morning, to my horror, I found myself in the other twenty percent. When I opened my eye, it was like looking at a Jackson Pollock painting: streaks and spots of black. I called the doctor's office right away and was scheduled for a second surgery that evening.

The dear doctor was so kind. This time, the operation took forty-five minutes and he lasered all around the area to prevent further tearing—as if he were mending socks! These operations do not hurt at all, but the vision is profoundly affected.

The worst part of my recovery was that I was instructed to keep my head down for a few weeks! There is a sort of "buckle" positioned in the retina to keep the whole thing intact, and you aren't supposed to raise your head except when putting in the various eye drops required. It was hell! I had to sleep in a certain position and make sure my head was down at all times. I tell you, I could not do it. I would try, but end up halfway on my side. I got so depressed that I'd throw head onto a pillow off and on, exhausted. My vision was distorted so that I saw wavy lines. My macula had been damaged and the vision in my right eye was now 120/20; everything was extremely blurry.

Throughout 2013, I was given injections for macular degeneration, but they did nothing to restore or improve my vision. One day, as I arrived for my appointment, the doctor had to go take care of an emergency so I asked if I could see Dr. Spaide, Medicare or not. I was informed that he did take Medicare now, and would see me.

Dr. Spaide looked at my eyes and declared, "You are a very interesting person! You have two different eyes, as if they are from two different people! It is as if one of them is twenty years older than the other. This is very unusual."

I felt like some kind of scientific specimen. "Two different eyes?" I said. "Maybe I have two different personalities, too!" I think he might have agreed. All he said in response was, "Hmm," and then, "We have to remove the scar tissue." This was a new angle!

It was decided that Dr. Spaide would perform the surgery, but first I had to have a cataract removed, which was in the way. He referred me to a Dr. Amilia Shrier at the Eye and Ear Hospital on the Upper East Side. Let me explain here that the front of the eye is one specialty and the back of the eye another, so they require the expertise of different doctors.

When I met Dr. Shrier, I could not believe how fortunate I was to be treated by her. She may be the warmest and most beautiful human being and doctor I have ever met. She hugged and comforted me, and called me her "macula lady." At 120/20, my right eye was in very bad shape and looked scary on the scans she showed me, but she thought that my first surgeon had done a good job of lasering the detached retina. "Ten years ago," she told me, "nothing could have been done."

Dr. Shrier performed the cataract surgery in December of 2013. The operation went very well, and shortly afterwards, at the beginning of 2014, Dr. Spaide performed the fourth surgery on my right eye, removing the scar tissue. My vision improved slowly and, after a few months, it was back to 20/20. My depression lifted and Dr. Spaide and Dr. Shrier were both quite pleased at the outcome. Dr. Shrier calls it a miracle every time she sees me.

I now get injections in my right eye for so-called wet macular degeneration. The thought of a needle in the eye scares the daylights out of people, but it is not as bad as it sounds. Numbing drops are administered first, and then the doctor gently applies a soft little clamp to the eyelid. The injection is a dull little stab, a bit like a flu shot, after which I sometimes see what look like black pearls or ocean waves in my field of vision. That's the medicine.

At one point, Dr. Spaide called me Superwoman, for all the procedures I had been through. He is a blunt and serious, a man of few words, but he possesses an understated sense of humor I appreciate. I think of him as the Super Surgeon who saved my eyesight.

It was now 2014, and Obama was our President. Looking back, I miss his civility, intelligence, and diplomatic demeanor. He will be remembered for those qualities, as well as for being the first African American President of the United States— and especially by some of us for passing the Affordable Care Act. It is now 2020 and we are facing another election. Think of all of those preexisting conditions before you vote this time. We may need to improve on the system we have, but we certainly shouldn't do away with it.

Once my eyes had been treated, I wanted to get out of New York for a little while. I needed the ocean breeze and the rustle of palm trees, so I flew Delta down to Florida, where my two Swedish friends lived in Jupiter. I have been to Florida many times over the previous few years, as well as a long time earlier, when I'd spent time in the Florida Keys. Back then, it was about fishing boats and inhabited by just the locals and a few seasonal residents who owned little houses. The main highway through the Keys was just a strip of road with the ocean on both sides, stretching from Key Largo all the way down to Key West. It was from there that Pan Am had flown its first flight ever—a mail carrier—to Havana, Cuba, in 1926.

Besides feeling the ocean breezes, I needed to celebrate my recuperation with lobster and stone crabs or soft shell crabs, yellowtail fish or grouper, wine, and key lime pie. I know the United States quite well. I lived in San Francisco,

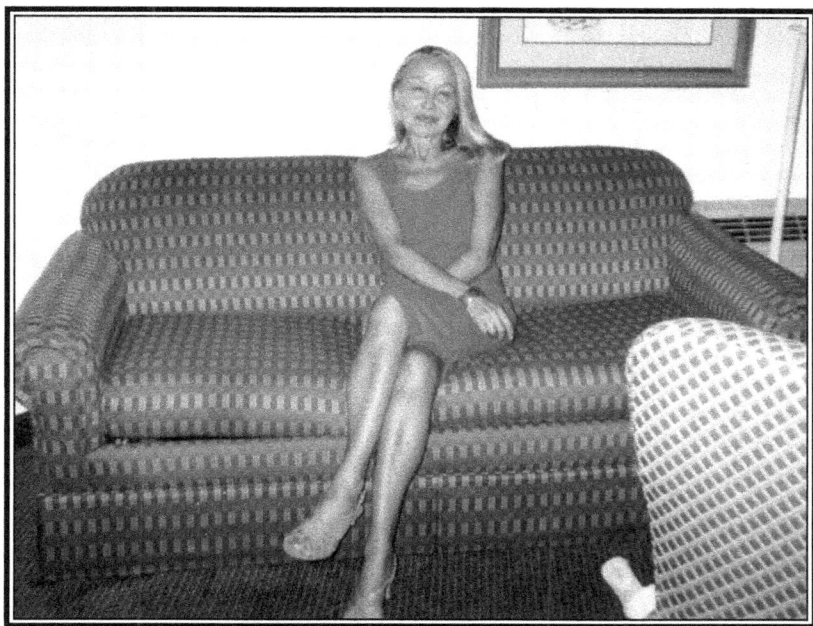

Relaxing in Florida.

visited family in Los Angeles, and have often visited the colorful South, including such cities as Atlanta and Birmingham. For the airline memorabilia shows I attend, I go to Chicago, New Jersey, Atlanta, Los Angeles, Houston, San Francisco, Cincinnati, Portland, Dallas, and more. How different one city is from another! It takes years to get to know the United States. It's said that today, our country is divided into two parts politically, but it seems much more complicated than that.

At Christmastime in 2014, my Swedish family came to visit me in New York—my brother Carl Gustaf and his partner Ulf, my nephew Gustaf and his wife Camilla, and their two sons. They marveled at the views from the three windows of the Jewel. My friend Eva, a long-time resident of New York and former Pan Am colleague, likes to prepare very fine Swedish Christmas dinners at her Upper East Side apartment.

Back in our Pan Am days, Eva would set up the first-class carts with special precision. I remember one time, we were in the galley and I spilled a drop of water the size of a pinhead on her cart. "No, no!" she said. "No messing up my cart!" "But…the passengers can't see that drop of water if they used a magnifying glass!" I replied. "OH, YES THEY CAN!" she insisted. That was Eva.

Another time, on a transatlantic flight when the crew in the main cabin insisted upon yet one more soft drink service after we'd completed five or six, Eva said, "What do they need THAT for?"

While I'm again on the subject of Pan Am, I have to mention a few words about that TV series *Pan Am* that aired a few years ago. I would be hard-pressed to find a more ludicrous and unrealistic production! Pan Am captains did not look like teenagers. And, with all due respect to the actors, the stewardesses did not behave like that. The uniforms of our TV coun-

Eva at one of her Christmas dinners.

terparts were too tight, their handbags were not Pan Am bags, their gloves and shoes were all wrong. We did not take a swig from a Champagne bottle. We had paper cups hidden away in the galley. Our famous girdles were not worn in bed. And beyond that, the sex scenes in the show were very staged and seemed quite phony!

"It's a TV show," some would say, and I understand that. But I think it could have been much more realistic and interest-

The family celebrating Carl Johan's seventy-fifth birthday.

ing. The only really authentic aspect of the show was the airplanes. And I do recall one scene that I thought was quite realistic. They were taking off from a risky, short runway and the two crew members in the jumpseats looked nervous and held on tight, strapped into their seatbelts. It's true that landings and takeoffs could be frightening, especially in bad weather.

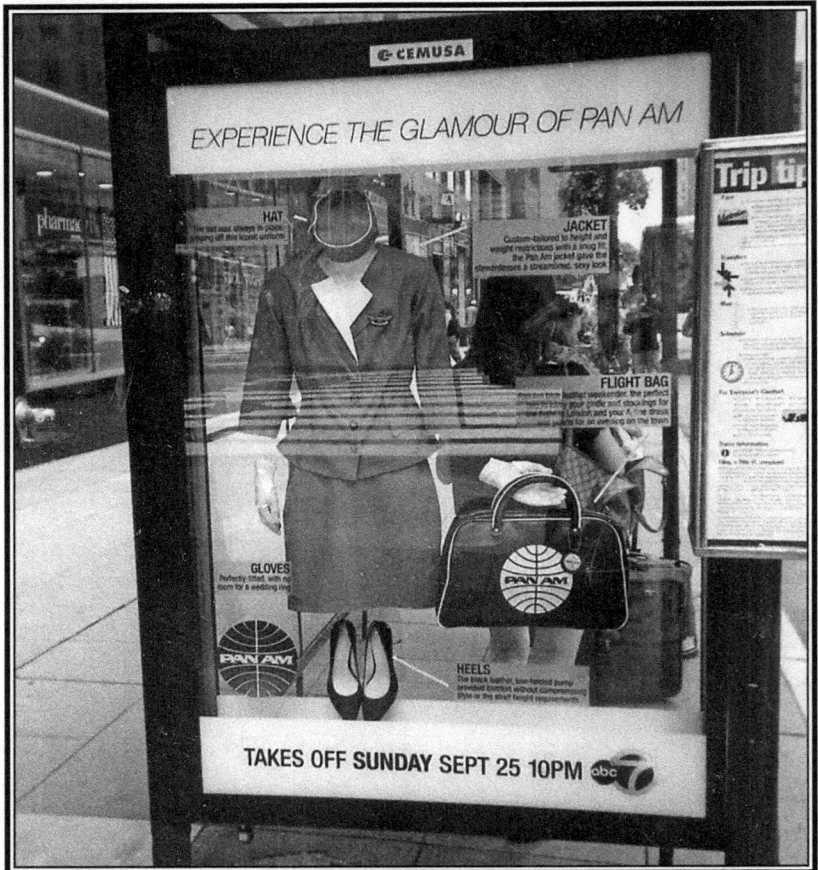

A bus stop ad for the TV drama about Pan Am.

During the six years I lived in the Jewel, New York became even more expensive and full of noisy construction sites. At one point, several renovations were taking place in my building simultaneously and, from my perch on the twenty-sixth floor, I could hear noise above, below, and beside me. This went on for years. Of course, upgrading apartments is a good thing and often necessary. But a person like me, who is retired and doesn't leave for work in the morning, is particularly inconvenienced by the construction noise.

I got the idea that if I sold my unit and bought one much higher up in the building, I could escape most of the drilling and demolition noise. The Woodstock Tower tapers off at the top like a wedding cake, so there are far fewer studios on the uppermost floors.

I started investigating the situation, looking around me and keeping track of what was selling. Several units are for sale at any given time in the Woodstock building, and this was where the formidable real estate broker, Donna Conti, with the firm Douglas Elliman, entered the scene. She lives in the building and I happened to meet her in the elevator, where we started a conversation. She agreed to come see my apartment.

"I can sell this!" she said, the minute she saw the Jewel. That was in 2017, and we put it on the market that spring.

Donna and I collaborated for a few months, showing the place to potential buyers, some of them serious and others not so serious. We got some offers, but I knew I'd have to have patience and wait for the right one. Meanwhile, I continually cleaned the apartment and put things away—even sold some stuff, including oriental carpets—to make the place look bigger and brighter.

We finally sold the Jewel to a very lovely gentleman, an American Filipino with an impressive resume who now lives here with the rest of us. It is Donna's job to scrutinize the buyer's financials, and she is *very* thorough, as she has to be in our rather fraudulent environment. Buying and selling can take three months or even longer if a mortgage is involved. Then there is the infamous closing. In Manhattan, every closing involves the buyer and buyer's agent, the seller and seller's agent, their respective attorneys, the bank lender, and the representative of the management company who conducts the proceedings. The process involves signing a lot of papers, and takes about two hours if there are no snags.

So, having sold the Jewel, what was I to do? Once again, I had no home and nowhere to go. (I hadn't been able to buy a new place before I'd sold the old one, because the board would want to see that I had the money ready to go.)

Donna and I decided I should rent a "parking space" in Woodstock Tower before I bought again. There were many rentals available, and she was gracious about accompanying me from one crummy-looking studio to another. One was furnished with ugly old furniture and had a broken window. Another was not yet available. A third one was just a mess. They were all going for about $2,000 a month, and were owned by tenant shareholders who had to pay a hefty percentage to the managing agent. On top of that, there were move-out fees, move-in fees, processing fees, flip taxes—you name it. Manhattan real estate would make anybody's head spin.

Donna and I finally settled on a place I dubbed "The Dungeon." Apartment Number Ten. The Dungeon was on the fourth floor, dark and gloomy, but clean, empty, and quite big, with three ample closets. The kitchen was old and a bit seedy, but the bathroom was fine—and that's important. It looked out over 42nd Street, where I hoped the traffic between First and Second Avenues wouldn't be too terrible. And, oh dear…the windows were dirty and the blinds even worse. I hate blinds because they break apart and are difficult to clean. I would find out soon enough that the old air-conditioner was noisy and clumsy, and of course it malfunctioned after a few months, as

"The Jewel" is sold!

did the refrigerator. Ah yes, New York!

No surprise when I spotted a water bug climbing up on a screen I had placed next to the kitchen. The I saw the second one sitting upright in the middle of the room staring at me. The third one was dead when I found it, and the

fourth one was half dead. The fifth and sixth were next to my bed! I wanted out of the Dungeon fast.

I was desperate to be high up and away from the creepy crawlers, away from the dirty and dark dungeon, away from the cars outside. And, oh yes, I forgot to mention the cold. There is plenty of heat in the building, but the wind was blowing right through my windows and even the wall. I placed pillows and towels around to block out the drafts, to little effect. There was one spot in particular where the cold continued to seep through.

Donna and I were on the prowl for my next real estate venture, and, in spite of my troubles with the Dungeon, I really loved the building. The staff is wonderful and all the people are, shall we say, civilized.

I went to all the showings on high floors. The places were too expensive, had so-so views, weren't high enough, required too much renovation, and so on. Then I met Lina Lee in the elevator. She occupied a very small studio on the 30th floor. There are thirty-two of them, but this particular unit, in spite of the diminutive size, had one great advantage: NO ONE ABOVE! And she wanted to sell.

Lina was a very sweet and well-educated young Chinese girl. Her parents lived in Queens and had bought the studio for her about two years earlier for a good price, but now she had a Wall Street job and wanted to move on in the world. Donna had shown me the place earlier, before I'd been ready to sell my Jewel. We took another look after four years.

Lina was a young girl with a lot of possessions, so Unit 3018, which was maybe eighteen feet by eight feet including the hallway, was a bit scruffy and messy. The hall needed some work, the walls were painted horrible colors, there was an awkward Murphy bed and a useless dishwasher—but in a renovated kitchen. The bathroom was old but okay. I decided to buy it.

It was time to sign yet another contract, and I called the attorney Donna had sent me to when I'd bought the Jewel. Lina and her parents owned the studio jointly, and had their own Chinese lawyer. It took a long time for them to sign the contract, and I was feeling the pressure of my one-year contract on the Dungeon, which was almost up.

Finally, everything was signed and Donna set about preparing all of my documents—financials, tax returns, reference letters—to present to the managing agent and board. The fact that I'd already lived in the building for eight years didn't seem to matter—but the director of the board was a very sympathetic man, and approved me quickly after the so-called board package had been accepted.

A closing date was set for early July 2018, but suddenly, dear Lina was not ready to move! The date was postponed for a few weeks, and then one afternoon, I got a call on the intercom from the desk. Lina and her mother wanted to see me. I let them into the Dungeon. They wanted to know how I would feel about postponing the closing for six months.

How would I feel? I went through the roof! I had been waiting for a little place on a high floor for four years, and now I was finally going to be at the very top, with no one above me. There was no other apartment like it. I wanted it right then, and there was no way would I wait six months!

Lina's mother was really very understanding. She relented right away, and the drama was over, except in Lina's mind. She still did not feel ready to move and she showed it. Nevertheless, a new closing date was set for end of July.

My lawyer was adamant that Lina vacate the place by the closing—no grace period. Four of us—Lina's mother, a member of the building staff, Donna, and I—assembled and moved out Lina's belongings.

That was the end of the problem for me, but the drama continued. When Lina refused to move in with her parents in Queens, Donna warmheartedly offered to let her sleep on her own couch for two weeks. Eventually, Lina got herself an apartment elsewhere in midtown.

Once I took occupancy of Apartment Number Eleven, what I called "The Little Tower," it was time for Tony, the formidable maintenance man, to upgrade it. Luckily, I could arrange to stay another two months in the Dungeon.

During that time, Tony removed all the ugly furniture and pulled the Murphy bed right out of the wall. He also took out two clumsy doors that were just in the way and all of the unnecessary shelves in the three closets. The dishwasher was thrown away and replaced with a fridge. Another small fridge went under the sink. Tony fixed the lights and installed special bulbs, put up curtain rods, and did lots of other little things. He truly was a miracle maintenance man. Once he'd painted the whole place white, it was bright and light, with a magnificent view from what felt like the top of the world.

My furniture, such as it was, was moved in. All I really had was a bed, a dresser, and a few paintings. I bought a beautiful gold-brown armchair. The older you get, the less you need. Inspired by my new perch in the sky, I renamed the place, "The Bird Nest."

When you buy a piece of real estate in the city, you are actually buying a little piece of Manhattan. People from other places tend to be stunned by the prices. Studios in good buildings go for $350-500,000 and one-bedrooms can be twice that. There's no getting around it. At this point, I have no intention of selling ever again. The Bird Nest is quiet, and I know that my friends and family are there for me, however scattered they might be geographically. You know from all my stories where they are. Then there are some who are real New Yorkers, like me, who have lived here thirty, forty, or even fifty years.

The Great Big Witch on the Hudson has its problems, but it is still very vibrant and has become an international mecca. It may not have the character it had in the seventies and eighties, but everything changes. Today, cyclists crowd the sidewalks and streets, running red lights shamelessly and riding against traffic. Cars, a lot of them Ubers and Lyfts, choke the intersections and cause gridlock. Pedestrians charge ahead, relentlessly staring at their iPhones, and almost causing accidents. Mothers plow the sidewalks with baby carriages, nearly mowing down slower walkers. Has the world gone mad? Only

The view from the thirtieth-floor "Bird Nest"—my final home in New York.

the loveable dogs of New York seem unperturbed as they stride along beside Mommy, Daddy, or the dog-walker.

I still have my Mr. X, a bond that has lasted for fifty years. As someone once said, you can't walk away from love.

Will 2020 turn out to be another milestone year? You've probably heard the French phrase, "*Plus que ca change, rien ne change.*" The United States is a country of perennial change, though. Groups of people come along who say they want to make things better. Everyone is always stirring things up, discussing, opining, arguing, and quarrelling. Well, these are the essential elements of our democracy, which I hope is alive and well. Just as it was in 1966, when I arrived here, the American Spirit remains unique and unquestionably positive.

It will be fifty-four years in April 2020 that I am in the USA, and I am still "Dancing around the Edge," but more slowly now!

www.ingramcontent.com/pod-product-compliance
Lightning Source LLC
Chambersburg PA
CBHW060300100426
42742CB00011B/1814